HELLO GOD
it's Me

me. In the meantime, my sister Ronda, persuaded me to purchase a good study Bible. So I did, but I didn't read it. Every night it was my habit to sit in the living room and read (anything but the Bible) after Merion went to bed. God was bothering me mightily to pick up that Bible and read it, but I resisted. I didn't realize at the time that it was the Holy Spirit relentlessly prodding my conscience. After several months I gave in, and started reading my Bible. God basically grabbed me by the collar and never let me go. I would read the Bible secretly every night. Secretly indeed, because I knew that if my wife knew I was reading the Bible, she would start bugging me to go to church with her. Well, Easter Sunday came around and Merion said to me, "How about we go to this little Christian Church over here this morning, come on, it's Easter Sunday." So, I went. After the service they asked for volunteers to help with the Children's Church. We both volunteered, and it has been a wonderful and blessed journey since then.

The purpose of this book is to provide a Biblical foundation of the truths regarding prayer, realizing that God's Word has given us a blueprint by which we can communicate with Him, availing ourselves to His power. And we want people to realize that yes, God really desires for us to call on Him and when we do, He will listen and answer our prayers.

This book is not intended to be an exhaustive theological essay or complicated study on prayer. Our intent is to provide simple, plain, clear guidelines and tools the reader can use to tap into a powerful and fruitful prayer life. Through this study, it is our hope that the reader will grow in their faith and confidence in God.

Why the King James Version?

The scope of this book is confined within the bounds of God's Holy Word – The Bible, and what He has to say about prayer in the Old and New Testament. We will be using the Authorized King James Version, Oxford UP, 1998.

God promised us that He would preserve His Word. God made *Himself* responsible for preserving them.

> *"The words of the Lord are pure words: as silver tried in a furnace of earth, purified seven times. Thou shalt keep them, O LORD, thou shalt preserve them from this generation for ever." (Ps. 12:6-7)*

> *"Heaven and earth shall pass away: but my words shall not pass away." (Matt. 24:35, Luke 21:33)*

Secondly, God holds *us* responsible for adding to or taking away from His Words.

> *"For I testify unto every man that heareth the words of the prophecy of this book, If any man shall add unto these things, God shall add unto him the plagues that are written in this book. And if any man shall take away from the words of the book of this prophecy, God shall take away his part out of the book of life, and out of the holy city, and from the things which are written in this book." (Rev. 22:18-19)*

Notice that the emphasis in this sober warning at the end of the Bible is on the very *words* of scripture, not the general thoughts.

The book, *51 Reasons Why the King James (Daniels, D.W., 2018),* tells us in 1604, God picked a man, King James VI of Scotland and I of England, to set the best scholars of Puritans and Anglicans to the task of making a single translation of the Old and New Testaments. Over 54 people in total had to agree over every word of every verse of 1189 chapters of the Bible. They went over every verse no less than 14 times, from 1604 to 1610, and then it was checked again for publication in 1611.

We believe that, in English, the King James Bible is a literal preservation of what God spoke to His prophets and apostles. This is a complex subject and some may argue this (Christians argue about everything, don't we?).

Dr. Donald Waite made the following excellent comment on this subject:

> *The Bible is not a first-grade primer. It is God's book. It is a book that must be diligently read. It is only by 'searching the Scriptures' that we find what pertains to life and death. It tells of creation, of the mighty universe, of the future or the past, of the Mighty God and His wonders, of the Holy Spirit's ministry among Christians, of the Son of God's great sacrifice for sin, of home in Heaven for the believer, and of a fiery hell for the unsaved. How dare we assume that His Word can be capsulated in a comic book [or a version that reads 'like the morning newspaper']. Some people say they like a particular version because 'it's more readable'. Now, readability is one thing, but does the readability conform to what's in the original Greek*

and Hebrew language? You can have a lot of readability, but if it doesn't match up with what God has said, it's of no profit. In the King James Bible, the words match what God has said. You may say it's difficult to read, but study it out. [At times it's] hard in the Hebrew and Greek and, perhaps, even in the English in the King James Bible. But to change it around just to make it simple, or interpreting it instead of translating it, is wrong. You've got lots of interpretation, but we don't want that in a translation. We want exactly what God said in the Hebrew or Greek brought over into English. (Waite, D., 2020)

God is perfectly capable of using language to convey to us what He wants us to know. The Bible is composed of the very words of God. With these words God is able to say what He means, and someday He will hold us accountable for believing what He says.

DEDICATION:

Although God has brought many people into our lives influencing us toward the truth of the gospel and the authority of His Word, we are most indebted to our wonderful Christian parents, David and Betty Jean Haworth who introduced us to Jesus at an early age.

This book is dedicated to our beloved children, Ryan, Zachary, and Jacob in the hope that they will experience the inexpressible joy of a close walk with God.

ACKNOWLEDGEMENTS

We wish to extend our sincere thanks and gratitude to Merion Haworth (Rex's beloved wife) for her tireless work in reviewing, editing and making suggestions for the manuscript.

We also wish to extend our thanks and gratitude to Ronda's husband Steve, for his encouragement, and holding down the fort.

INTRODUCTION:

ALL OF US BECOME DISCOURAGED IN LIFE, FEELING THERE is no one to help us, listen or care. Few people would disagree that life is a hard road, it is. Just when we think things are going well and we think we're doing all the right things; a monkey wrench comes flying in from nowhere and messes everything up and down we go. A few years ago, I (Rex) was flying along on cloud nine. Yes sir, I had it figured out. The kids were grown and out of the house, the mortgage was almost paid and financial security was becoming a reality. Then the doctor said, "You have cancer." What? You've got to be kidding. I didn't drink; smoke and I thought I ate a good diet. Well, it happened anyway. Maybe I don't have control. Someone else is in charge. Although I did all of the chemotherapy, surgery and radiation, I knew ultimately it was up to God whether I stick around on this earth a while longer or not. From day one of my diagnosis, my loved ones, my local church and extended prayer communities cried out to God on my behalf. They prayed.

And personally, although our pastor is a great preacher, the best preacher I ever heard was cancer. Maybe a little wakeup call? Was God saying, "I want you to be completely dependent on me"?

"Draw nigh to God, and he will draw nigh to you…"
(James 4:8)

Disease has a way of changing your perspective and rearranging your priorities. For others it may be financial disaster, addiction, broken relationships, or some other calamity. Suddenly prayer became more important. It wasn't just a daily habit, a quick "praise the Lord and pass the potatoes". *It was my lifeline.*

So why are we writing this book on prayer? Because we've both been drastically humbled, become extremely dependent, and have desperately cried out to God. We have experienced the grace and power of prayer and we want to share this with you.

"Come unto me, all ye that labour and are heavy laden,
and I will give you rest." (Matt. 11:28)

Have you been at this point in your life? You're discouraged or maybe even down for the count, your luck is up, and your options have run out. There *is* someone there for you, someone who deeply cares and loves you, someone who wants to have a personal relationship with you, someone who is ready to throw you a lifeline, to reach down and pull you out of this mess. This "someone" is God, who came in the flesh, the God/Man Jesus Christ.

Some people think they can go to Heaven because they are a good person. Good compared to whom, your neighbor or the president of the PTA? You may consider yourself to be a good person but God's standard is perfection. He knew we could never reach that standard. That's why Jesus came to earth, the perfect Lamb of God.

"For all have sinned, and come short of the glory of God."
(Rom. 3:23)

"For the wages of sin is death; but the gift of God is
eternal life through Jesus Christ our Lord." (Rom. 6:23)

There will be no bragging in Heaven. We cannot be saved by our own works or righteousness, but only by God's grace through faith. Faith is not "trying", faith is trusting and believing. Faith is a gift!

"For by grace are ye saved through faith; and that not of
yourselves: it is the gift of God: Not of works, lest any
man should boast." (Eph. 2:8-9)

The cross of Jesus is the bridge between God and man. All we have to do is open our hearts and *believe.*

"Behold, I stand at the door,
and knock: if any man hear
my voice, and open the door,
I will come in to him, and
will sup with him, and he
with me." (Rev. 3:20)

"For God so loved the
world, that he gave his
only begotten Son, that

"Behold I stand at the
door and knock..."

*whosoever believeth in him should not perish but have
everlasting life." (John 3:16)*

Once we *believe* the gospel, God gives us His Holy Spirit to live
in us, never to leave us. The Holy Spirit teaches us and brings His
Word to our minds giving us truth, wisdom and knowledge. He
gives us peace and lack of fear, and He is our comforter and helper.

*"And I will pray the Father, and he shall give you
another Comforter, that he may abide with you for
ever; Even the Spirit of truth; whom the world cannot
receive, because it seeth him not, neither knoweth him:
but ye know him; for he dwelleth with you, and shall
be in you." (John 14:16-17)*

*We are saved by Grace alone
Through Faith alone
In Jesus Christ alone
According to the Scripture alone
To the Glory of God alone*

TABLE OF CONTENTS

Chapter One

WHAT IS PRAYER? WHY DO IT?

"Our greatest outlet of spiritual power is prayer. I can do more for God through prayer than I can do through any other means, including service." (Smith, C., 2020)

What is prayer?

PRAYER IS ACCESS TO GOD THE FATHER THROUGH JESUS Christ. There are many people today who falsely believe that God is an "impersonal undifferentiated Oneness", not separate from creation (evolutionary pantheism, frequently expressed in "New Age" philosophy). However, the truth is God is the only God, He is the eternal God, God is the creator God. He is *not a part* of creation; He made and designed all things. He is outside of time. There was no "before" God created. There was not even "nothing"! There was God existing in eternity.

"Before the mountains were brought forth, or ever thou hadst formed the earth and the world, even from everlasting to everlasting, thou art God." (Ps. 90:2)

Jesus is the image of God and the first born of every creature. By Him all things were created.

> *"All things were made by him; and without him was not any thing made that was made." (John 1:3)*

We must recognize who God is before we pray, and who we are before Him. The prayer of salvation is the ONE prayer He will hear from those who are not Christ believers. When we come to God and ask Him for something, it is futile if we don't have a personal relationship with Jesus.

> *"Jesus saith unto him, I am the way, the truth, and the life: no man cometh unto the Father but by me." (John 14:6)*
>
> Romans 10:9 says, *"That if thou shalt confess with thy mouth the Lord Jesus, and shalt believe in thine heart that God hath raised him from the dead, thou shalt be saved."*

God says when we pray individually, we should find a quiet place free from noise and distractions, and pray to the Father in secret. We don't need to be concerned about using many words or even specific words, because He knows what we need before we ask Him.

> In Matthew 6:6-8, Jesus says, *"But thou, when thou prayest, enter into thy closet, and when thou hast shut thy door, pray to thy Father which is in secret; and thy Father which seeth in secret shall reward thee openly.*

> *But when ye pray, use not vain repetitions, as the hea-*
> *then do: for they think that they shall be heard for their*
> *much speaking. Be not ye therefore like unto them: for*
> *your Father knoweth what things ye have need of,*
> *before ye ask him."*

However, God hears our prayers wherever we are. It is the attitude of our heart that is important. Scripture tells us, *"for the LORD seeth not as man seeth; for man looketh on the outward appearance, but the LORD looketh on the heart". (I Sam. 16:7b)*

Some people pray while driving in their car, others pray when they go for a walk, some have a special chair or even a prayer room and some of us pray in the midst of our daily lives. It makes no difference where or when you pray. Prayer is the key to unlocking *God's* prevailing power in our lives. God's power flows freely to people who pray. That power may come in the form of wisdom, patience, courage, confidence, self-control, perseverance, a changed attitude toward someone, a changed circumstance, or maybe an outright miracle.

> *Prayer is discourse with the personal God Himself. There*
> *in the act and dynamic of praying, I bring my whole life*
> *under His gaze. Yes, He knows what is in my mind, but*
> *I still have the privilege of articulating to Him what is*
> *there. He says, "Come, Speak to Me. Make your requests*
> *known to Me." And so, we come in order to know Him*
> *and to be known by Him.* (Sproul, R.C., 1984)

Prayer is the most personal way to *experience God*, to encounter Him and to grow in knowledge of Him. According to the book of Ephesians, God's desire is for *us* to be ***"Praying always with all prayer and supplication in the Spirit…" (Eph 6:18).***

> *"We must ask that we may receive: but that we should receive what we ask in respect of our lower needs, is not God's end in making us pray, for He could give us every-thing without that: to bring His child to his knee, God withholds that man may ask."* (MacDonald, G., 1947)

When we work, we work. But when we pray, God works! In 2 Chronicles 20, a great army came against the Southern Kingdom of Judah. King Jehoshaphat feared and proclaimed a fast for all of Judah to pray for help from the Lord. They had no strength to come up against this great army. King Jehoshaphat bowed his face to the ground and all Judah fell and prayed before the Lord, praising and singing to God. In answer, the Lord sent an ambush against the children of Ammon, Moab and Mt. Seir and they destroyed one another.

We, as Christians are God's children and joint-heirs with Jesus Christ.

Saint Paul, in his letter to the Ephesians writes,

> ***"Having predestined us unto the adoption of children by Jesus Christ to himself, according to the good pleasure of his will." (Eph. 1:5)***

Romans 8:16-17 says, ***"The Spirit itself beareth wit-ness with our spirit, that we are the children of God: And if children, then heirs; heirs of God, and joint-heirs*** *with Christ; if so be that we suffer with him, that we may be also glorified together."*

God has adopted us as His own children and this is not of our doing, but through the finished work of Jesus Christ on the cross. We come into His family and we share great treasures as co-heirs of his best gifts; His Son, forgiveness and eternal life. With this strong relationship, He encourages us to ask Him for whatever we need. How awesome is that!

And, the Bible teaches that God is looking for opportunities to pour out His blessings on us and give us good gifts. In a beautiful passage in Deuteronomy God promises,

> *"And all these blessings shall come on thee and over-take thee, that thou shalt harken unto the voice of the LORD thy God. Blessed shalt thou be in the city and blessed shalt thou be in the field. Blessed shall be the fruit of thy body and the fruit of thy ground and the fruit of thy cattle, the increase of thy kine, and the flocks of thy sheep. Blessed shall be thy basket and thy store. Blessed shalt thou be when thou comest in, and blessed shalt thou be when thou goest out." (Deut. 28:2-6)*

Matthew 7:9-11, Jesus says, *"Or what man is there of you, whom if his son ask bread, will he give him a stone? Or if he ask a fish, will he give him a serpent? If ye then, being evil, know how to give good gifts unto your children, how much more shall your Father which is in heaven give good things to them that ask him?"*

We are blessed beyond measure by God in our lives. Jesus shows us the heart of the Father. He is loving, He understands and cares about us. If sinful and fallible human beings can be kind, imagine how kind the Holy and perfect God is, the Creator of kindness. He is the good Father!

> *"...The LORD, the LORD God, merciful and gracious, longsuffering, and abundant in goodness and truth." (Exod. 34:6)*

PRAYER - Our Part - G.A.R.

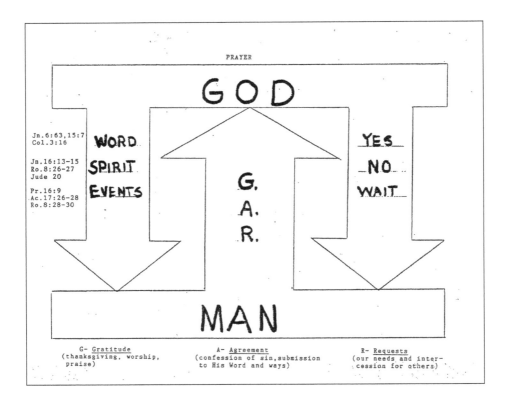

Gratitude:

Gratitude expresses thankfulness and praise in both trials and blessings of life. Because of our selfish, self-centered nature, we as humans tend to prefer the "gimme" part instead of the thankful part. It's easy to be grateful for some *thing* we receive or are given, like when a friend offers to pick up the check at lunch. We all have our list of things we want God to do for us, our list of things we want and the things we want Him to get rid of. But when we pray and give thanks to God, even when it's hard to, He promises us grace and faith, peace and joy. Gratitude includes worship. Sometimes in the midst of praying for our needs, the last thing we are thinking of is worshipping God.

We thank God for listening to us, but we need to stop and think about just whom we are in the presence of - His Perfect Holiness, waiting on Him, and worshipping Him. He says, *"Be still, and know that I am God…" (Ps. 46:10).* And in our stillness, in our pain, in the dark, when we are falling apart, when we don't understand, we must worship Him.

> *"Oh LORD our Lord, how excellent is thy name in all the earth! Who hast set thy glory above the heavens. Out of the mouth of babes and sucklings hast thou ordained strength because of thine enemies, that thou mightest still the enemy and the avenger. When I consider thy heavens, the work of thy fingers, the moon and the stars, which thou hast ordained; What is man, that thou art mindful of him? and the son of man, that thou visitest him? For thou hast made him a little lower than the angels, and hast crowned him with glory and honour. Thou madest*

him to have dominion over the works of thy hands; thou hast put all things under his feet: All sheep and oxen, yea, and the beasts of the field; The fowl of the air, and the fish of the sea, and whatsoever passeth through the paths of the seas. Oh LORD our Lord, how excellent is thy name in all the earth!" (Psalm 8)

Agreement:

Agreement is an attitude of harmony with God expressing His perfect Holiness and authority; that what He tells us in His Word is true. It includes confession of sin, and *turning* (to repent) from our own ways, *turning* and submitting to Him.

"If we confess our sins, he is faithful and just to forgive us our sins, and to cleanse us from all unrighteousness."
(1 John 1:9)

"If we confess our sins…"

Agreement is also acknowledging God knows what He's doing and submitting to His will. For example, in response to God's speech Job humbles himself:

> *"Then Job answered the LORD, and said, I know that thou canst do every thing, and that no thought can be withholden from thee. Who is he that hideth counsel without knowledge? therefore, have I uttered that I understood not; things too wonderful for me, which I knew not. Hear, I beseech thee, and I will speak: I will demand of thee, and declare thou unto me. I have heard of thee by the hearing of the ear: but now mine eye seeth thee. Wherefore I abhor myself, and repent in dust and ashes." (Job 42:1-6)*

Requests:

Requests include our needs and intercession for others. God invites us to ask Him and Jesus tells us in Matthew 7:7-8, *"Ask, and it shall be given you; seek, and ye shall find; knock and it shall be opened unto you: for everyone that asketh receiveth; and he that seeketh findeth; and to him that knocketh it shall be opened."* And in James 4:2b-3, *"ye have not, because ye ask not. Ye ask, and receive not, because ye ask amiss, that ye may consume it upon your lusts."* We have every opportunity, 24/7 to come to God, bring our requests to Him and look forward in faith to Him answering.

As we bring our requests to Him, He promises us to:

"Be careful for nothing; but in everything by prayer and supplication with thanksgiving let your requests be made known unto God. And the peace of God, which passeth all understanding, shall keep your hearts and minds through Christ Jesus." (Phil. 4:6-7)

"Be careful for nothing...but in everything pray."

What an amazing promise from our Heavenly Father!

When we ask believing in Him, trusting Him and aligning ourselves with Him, He says,

"And whatsoever ye shall ask in my name, that will I do, that the Father may be glorified in the Son. If ye shall ask any thing in my name, I will do it." (John 14:13-14)

PRAYER - God's Part - God answers our prayers by:

The Word:

The Word is the written Word (the Bible) and the Living Word, Jesus Christ.

> *"The Bible is the most offensive book ever written. It damns the whole human race. No one escapes."* (MacArthur, J., 2020)

> **The written Word** is the Bible, God's Holy Word, comprised of the Old and New Testaments. God's Word is alive!

> *"For the word of God is quick, and powerful, and sharper than any two-edged sword, piercing even to the dividing asunder of soul and spirit, and of the joints and marrow, and is a discerner of the thoughts and intents of the heart." (Heb. 4:12)*

> *"So shall my word be that goeth forth out of my mouth: it shall not return unto me void, but it shall accomplish that which I please, and it shall prosper in the thing whereto I sent it." (Isa. 55:11)*

> *"Thy word is a lamp unto my feet, and a light unto my path." (Ps. 119:105)*

The Living Word:

The Living Word is Jesus Christ who came to earth, lived among us, died for our sins and returned to Heaven, seated at the right hand of the throne of God the Father. He was in the beginning and is now and forevermore.

> *"In the beginning was the Word, and the Word was with God and the Word was God. The same was in the beginning with God. And the Word was made flesh, and dwelt among us, (and we beheld his glory, the glory as of the only begotten of the Father) full of grace and truth." (John 1:1-2, 14)*

> *"That which was from the beginning, which we have heard, which we have seen with our eyes, which we have looked upon, and our hands have handled, of the Word of life; (For the life was manifested, and we have seen it, and bear witness, and shew unto you that eternal life, which was with the Father, and was manifested unto us.)" (1 John 1:1-2)*

The Spirit:

The Spirit is the third Person of the Trinity. He is described in God's Holy Word as our comforter, counselor, and helper, guiding us into all truth. The Holy Spirit lives in us when we receive Jesus as our Lord and Savior! Jesus told his disciples that He was leaving them but the Holy Spirit was coming to live with and in them and said to them:

"And I will pray the Father, and he shall give you another Comforter, that he may abide with you for ever; Even the Spirit of truth; whom the world cannot receive, because it seeth him not, neither knoweth him; but ye know him; for he dwelleth with you and shall be in you." (John 14:16-17)

In John 16:13 it says,

"Howbeit when he, the Spirit of truth, is come, he will guide you into all truth: for he shall not speak of himself; but whatsoever he shall hear, that shall he speak: and he will shew you things to come." (John 16:13)

When we pray, the Spirit intercedes for us even when we are at a loss, confused, and can't think straight.

"Likewise the Spirit also helpeth our infirmities; for we know not what we should pray for as we ought; but the Spirit itself maketh intercession for us with groanings which cannot be uttered. And he that searcheth the hearts knoweth what is the mind of the Spirit because he maketh intercession for the saints according to the will of God." (Rom. 8:26-27)

When my brother Rex, was diagnosed with cancer, I was so shocked and distraught, I didn't even know how to pray. I cried a lot and pleaded to God to save him. But the Spirit knew what prayers my brother needed and what prayers my family needed and as we all sought Him, God began answering by giving us increased peace, patience, and faith. It was a long process of treatment, but through it all, the Holy Spirit comforted us, and guided our ideas about the outcome. My brother survived all the interventions and we are enjoying each day as a gift from the Lord.

In the Book of Job, Elihu is speaking to Job. Although Job's friends did not always give him good advice, there were times they did speak the truth. In the following verse, Elihu recognizes the truth that God is the only source of true wisdom when he said, *"but there is a spirit in man: and the inspiration of the Almighty giveth them understanding" (Job 32:8).*

> *What the church needs today is not more machinery, or better, not new organizations or more and novel methods, but men whom the Holy Ghost can use – men of prayer, men mighty in prayer. The Holy Ghost does not flow through methods, but through men. He does not come on machinery, but on men. He does not anoint plans, but men – men of prayer.* (Bounds, E.M., 1910)

Events:

Events in our lives are another way God answers prayers, demonstrating Himself by *doing* things!

The Painter's Answered Prayer

> *"A painter slipped and fell while working on a roof. Just as he rolled over the edge, he shouted, 'God help me!' Almost immediately his overalls caught on a nail and he found himself hanging just below the gutter. Reaching up to pull*

himself back onto the roof, he said 'never mind God, this nail caught me'." (Anonymous)

Like the painter, do you miss what God is doing?

Many times, in spite of our well-intended planning, merciful God orders, guides and directs our steps.

"A man's heart deviseth his way: but the Lord directeth his steps." (Prov. 16:9)

"Thou hast enlarged my steps under me, that my feet did not slip." (Ps. 18:36)

"The Lord directs his steps..."

In Acts 12, the church was praying without ceasing for Peter, whom Herod had thrown into prison. In response to those prayers, the Angel of the Lord came and released Peter from prison; chains fell off and iron prison gates opened as the Angel delivered Peter from the hand of Herod. The praying ones were astonished to see him! God answered their prayers with this remarkable and miraculous event.

I Chronicles 4 tells the story of Jabez. His mother named him Jabez because she bore him in sorrow, but Jabez called on God asking Him and saying, *"Oh, that thou wouldest bless me indeed, and enlarge my coast, that thine hand might be with me, and that thou wouldest keep me from evil, that it may not grieve me."* A simple prayer, but God granted him what he requested!

Why Do It?

> *"I pray because I can't help myself. I pray because I'm helpless. I pray because the need flows out of me all the time – waking and sleeping. It does not change God – it changes me."* (Lewis, C.S., 2018)

The greatest reason to pray is to come to salvation through Jesus Christ our Lord. As *believers*, here are some reasons we should pray:

God calls us to pray!

> *"Call unto me, and I will answer thee, and shew thee great and mighty things which thou knowest not."* (Jer. *33:3 - frequently referred to as God's telephone number.*)

"And he (Jesus) spake a parable unto them to this end, that men ought always to pray and not to faint." *(Luke 18:1)*

Jesus prayed regularly and instructs us to pray!

"And when he had sent the multitudes away, he went up into a mountain apart to pray: and when the evening was come, he was there alone." (Matt. 14:23)

"Watch and pray, that ye enter not into temptation: the spirit indeed is willing, but the flesh is weak." (Matt. 26:41)

"Prayer is not optional for the Christian; it is required." (Sproul, R.C., 1984)

He assumes we will pray!

"And when [not if] *thou prayest, thou shalt not be as the hypocrites are: for they love to pray standing in the synagogues and in the corners of the streets, that they may be seen of men. Verily I say unto you, They have their reward. But thou, when thou prayest, enter into thy closet, and when thou hast shut thy door, pray to thy Father which is in secret; and thy Father which seeth in secret shall reward thee openly." (Matt. 6:5-6)*

"Be careful for nothing; but in every thing by prayer and supplication with thanksgiving let your requests be made known unto God." (Phil. 4:6)

Prayer is how we communicate with God!

Someday we will see and speak with Him face to face, but until then, prayer is how we communicate with God.

"Thou shalt make thy prayer unto him, and he shall hear thee…" (Job 22:27)

"For we have not an high priest which cannot be touched with a feeling of our infirmities; but was in all points tempted like as we are, yet without sin. Let us therefore come boldly unto the throne of grace, that we may obtain mercy, and find grace to help in time of need." (Heb. 4:15-16)

As we spend time with Him, we are not only to ask and tell, but *listen.* He speaks to us and we hear from Him in many ways!

<u>Through His Word</u>:

"So then faith cometh by hearing, and hearing by the word of God." (Rom. 10:17)

"Faith comes by hearing the Word of God..."

To fully understand His communication with us, we must diligently read, study, and meditate upon His Word. God is whispering, and sometimes shouting, all through His Word, giving us instructions and principles for life. When we interpret Scripture by other Scripture, we avoid the false logic and misinterpretations that sneak into our world. If someone claims, "God told me to go kill my neighbor!" would you believe him? Of course not! God never violates His own Word or principles. That "voice" does not belong to God.

> Proverbs 3:5-6, ***"Trust in the LORD with all thine heart; and lean not unto thy own understanding. In all thy ways acknowledge him, and he shall direct thy paths."***

We must always be aware of the "voices" we listen to because we can fall into the deception of the Evil One.

"Be sober, be vigilant; because your adversary the devil, as a roaring lion, walketh about, seeking whom he may devour." (1 Pet. 5:8)

Through the Holy Spirit:

The Holy Spirit's job is to convict us of sin so we can become more like Jesus. He exchanges our sin for His righteousness (2 Corinthians 5:21) so we can be His hands and feet in the world today. What a comfort! What a privilege!

John 14:26, *"But the Comforter, which is the Holy Ghost, whom the Father will send in my name, he shall teach you all things, and bring all things to your remembrance, whatsoever I have said unto you."*

Through Music:

There is an undeniable link between the Holy Spirit and certain types of music. When I (Ronda) am needing to draw near to God and open my heart to His, I get alone somewhere and turn on my favorite praise and worship music and inevitably, my mood changes and my attitude is adjusted to being thankful and joyful!

A classic example of this is found in the Old Testament story of Elisha. This fierce prophet became part of an army that was on its way to attack the nation of Moab. After marching seven days and finding no water along the way, things became desperate. It looked as though the Israelites would all die before they ever arrived for the battle. Jehoshaphat, king of Judah heard Elisha was among them, and appealed to the prophet to do something.

In 2 Kings 3:15 Scripture tells us, the old prophet Elisha demanded, *"But now bring me a minstrel."* A minstrel was brought. *"And it came to pass, when the minstrel played, that the hand of the LORD came upon him."* Elisha told them to dig ditches, for a flood of water was soon to follow.

This passage is truly amazing. When the musician played, the Spirit moved. The Holy Spirit likes good music! His power is released, His mind is known, and His presence is felt when the right type of music is played (and sung).

Through the Wisdom of Others:

One of the ways in which you can hear the voice of the Holy Spirit is through the wise advice of others. Wise and knowledgeable people are invaluable.

"There is gold, and a multitude of rubies: but the lips of knowledge are a precious jewel." (Prov. 20:15)

My dear friend, Mary practices this. When she has an important decision to make, big or small, she seeks advice from those close to her who are walking with the Lord, then she takes that counsel again to God with a humble heart and asks for His leading. For some of us, it is difficult to ask others their advice. *"The way of a fool is right in his own eyes: but he that hearkeneth unto counsel is wise" (Prov. 12:15).* Prayerfully seek the Lord, reach out to people in your life who can speak the Truth through the Holy Spirit.

<u>Through His Creation:</u>

God speaking through creation or nature means that when we look up at the stars or gaze at mountains covered with tall pine trees and wildflowers, we see the fingerprints of God. The more we fix our eyes on the wonder of creation, the more we must conclude that these things couldn't happen by chance. God is surely and artist without any peer. The feelings of awe that come over us as we watch the waves pound against the rocks at the beach or hold a newborn baby for the first time are in fact God speaking to us through His masterpiece.

> Psalm 19:1-4 puts it this way, *"The heavens declare the glory of God; and the firmament sheweth his handywork. Day unto day uttereth speech, and night unto night sheweth knowledge. There is no speech nor language, where their voice is not heard. Their line is gone out through all the earth, and their words to the end of the world..."*

We also pray because we need renewed strength so we will not give up! God wants us to persevere and be persistent.

> *"But they that wait upon the LORD shall renew their strength; they shall mount up with wings as eagles; they shall run, and not be weary; and they shall walk, and not faint." (Isa. 40:31)*

In Luke 18:1-8, Jesus was teaching his disciples,

> *"And he spake a parable unto them to this end, that men ought always to pray, and not to faint; Saying, There was in a city a judge, which feared not God, neither regarded man: And there was a widow in that city; and she came unto him, saying, Avenge me of mine adversary. And he would not for a while: but afterword he said within himself, Though I fear not God, nor regard man; Yet because this widow troubleth me, I will avenge her lest by her continual coming she weary me. And the Lord said, Hear what the unjust judge sayeth. And shall not God avenge his own elect, which cry day and night unto him, though he bear long with them? I tell you that he will avenge them speedily. Nevertheless when the Son of man cometh, shall he find faith on the earth?"*

This example clearly illustrates that we really can't bug God too much - so persevere and *pray on!*

One of our favorite stories is about George Mueller. He prayed 60 years for the conversion of a friend. When Mueller died, that man was still unsaved. But a few weeks later, the old man turned to Christ. George Mueller might have felt God was not answering his prayers, but all the time the answer had been, "Yes, but not yet."

> *We have but to pray! All things are possible to us! Pray, Brothers and Sisters! You have the key in the door of Heaven, keep it there, and turn it till the gate shall open. Pray, Brethren, for prayer holds the chain which binds*

the old dragon! Prayer can hold fast and restrain even Satan himself! Pray! God girds you with Omnipotence if you know how to pray! May we not fail here, but may the Spirit of God strengthen us, and to God shall be Glory forever and ever. Amen. (Spurgeon, C.H., 1872)

Our prayers are precious to God and He says they are,

"...golden vials full of odours, which are the prayers of saints." (Rev. 5:8)

Chapter 2

HOW TO PRAY

Prayer does *change things, all kinds of things. But the most important thing it changes is us. As we engage in this communion with God more deeply and come to know the One with whom we are speaking more intimately, that growing knowledge of God reveals to us all the more brilliantly who we are and our need to change in conformity to Him. Prayer changes us profoundly.* (Sproul, R.C., 2009*)*

The Lord's Prayer

Matthew 6:9-13
"After this manner, therefore pray ye:
'Our Father which art in heaven,
Hallowed be thy name,
Thy kingdom come,
Thy will be done,
        in earth, as it is in heaven.
Give us this day our daily bread.

And forgive us our debts,
    as we forgive our debtors.
And lead us not into temptation,
    but deliver us from evil: For thine is the kingdom, the power, and
the glory, forever. Amen."

THIS IS A PATTERN — NOT AN EXAMPLE OF EXACT WORDS we must use. In the Lord's Prayer, Christ gives us an incomparable model for all prayer. It teaches that:

- Right prayer begins with worship
- The interest of the Kingdom comes before personal interest
- We are to accept the Father's will, whether to grant or withhold
- We are to petition for our present needs, leaving the future to the Father's care and love

There are 5 distinctive *characteristics* of the Lord's Prayer:

1. **It defines the attitude of the heart in which we should pray.** The attitude of our heart is more important than words or posture.

    "For all those things hath mine hand made, and all those things have been, saith the LORD; but to this man will I look, even to him that is poor and of a contrite spirit, and trembleth at my word." (Isa. 66:2)

The Hebrew word for *contrite* means to be crushed, or sometimes to be thoroughly crushed; to be dejected; broken; beaten to pieces, or broken into pieces; to be bruised; to be humbled (Strong, J., 1890).

2. **It is brief yet profound: there are 6 petitions and 35 words.** Prayers need not be lengthy in order to be effective.

   "But when he saw the wind boisterous, he was afraid; and, beginning to sink, he cried, saying, Lord, save me." (Matt. 14:30)

   "...for God is in heaven and thou upon earth: therefore, let thy words be few." (Eccles. 5:2b)

3. **It is wonderfully comprehensive**: It summarizes all that we should pray for.
4. **It has universal application**: It covers all needs common to humanity.
5. **It reveals priorities to be observed in prayer**: The prayer is half way through before the needs and desires of the petitioner are mentioned.

The Prayer:

"Our Father Which Art in Heaven"

When Christians bow before God and call Him Father, they are acknowledging that at the heart of the universe there is not only ultimate power but ultimate love. But not everyone can call God "Father". The relationship that we have with God as our Father comes only through our relationship with Jesus Christ. (Robinson, H., 1982)

It is a wonderful privilege to call God, "Father".

> *"Jesus saith unto him, 'I am the way, the truth, and the life; no man cometh unto the Father, but by me."* *(John 14:6)*

> *"But as many as received him, to them gave he power to become the sons of God, even to them that believe on his name." (John 1:12)*

The Old Testament saints and prophets referred to God as Father no more than 10 times (Wilson, R.F., 2020). Yet in the New Testament, hundreds of times Jesus and the disciples instruct believers to refer to God as *God the Father.*

> *"For ye have not received the spirit of bondage again to fear; but ye have received the Spirit of adoption, whereby we cry Abba, Father." (Rom. 8:15)*

Abba (Greek) is often understood to mean daddy or papa.

<u>Three Petitions Concerning God and His Glory:</u>

1. **"Hallowed Be Thy Name"**

   God's name represents His nature. To hallow is to treat holy; hold in reverence. This phrase is asking that His name be held universally and perpetually in reverence.

"Neither shall ye profane my holy name; but I will be hallowed among the children of Israel; I am the LORD which hallow you." (Lev. 22:32)

"Hallowed (Greek) means holy, set apart, sanctify, consecrate." (Strong, J., 1890)

"Therefore say unto the house of Israel, Thus sayeth the LORD God; I do not this for your sakes, O house of Israel, but for mine holy name's sake, which ye have profaned among the heathen, whither ye went. And I will sanctify my great name, which was profaned among the heathen, which ye hath profaned in the midst of them; and the heathen shall know that I am the LORD, sayeth the LORD God, when I shall be sanctified in you before their eyes." (Ezek. 36:22-23)

When we pray "hallowed be thy name" we are in an attitude of worship, and praise, exalting God and focusing on His character, *"I will praise thee, O Lord, among the people: I will sing unto thee among the nations. For thy mercy is great unto the heavens, and thy truth unto the clouds. Be thou exalted, O God, above the heavens: let thy glory be above all the earth" (Ps. 57:9-11).* We hallow God's name by receiving Him into our hearts and filling our minds with His Word.

The real crisis of worship today is not that the preaching is paltry or that's it's too drafty in church. It is that people have no sense of the presence of God, and if they have no sense of His presence, how can they be moved to express the deepest feelings of their soul, to honor, revere, worship and glorify God? (Sproul, R.C., 2009)

2. "Thy Kingdom Come"

The word kingdom here means 'reign'. This petition is an expression of our wish that God may reign everywhere, that His laws may be obeyed; and especially that the gospel of Christ may be advanced everywhere, **"and let the whole earth be filled with his glory; Amen, and Amen" (Ps. 72:19).**

When we pray "thy kingdom come" we are agreeing that our purpose as believers is to bring His Kingdom into our everyday lives by surrendering to His Kingship. Every thought, every word, every action is brought under His reign. He is Master of the Universe.

But He's Coming Back!

The verb "come" describes a climactic, not gradual, coming of His kingdom. As believers, we are to pray and watch for the coming of His kingdom and the ultimate reign of Christ, the King of Kings and Lord or Lords!

> *"And I saw heaven opened, and behold a white horse; and he that sat upon him was called Faithful and True, and in righteousness he doth judge and make war. His eyes were as a flame of fire, and on his head were many crowns; and he had a name written, that no man knew, but he himself. And he was clothed with a vesture dipped in blood; and his name is called The*

Word of God. And the armies which were in heaven followed him upon white horses, clothed in fine linen, white and clean. And out of his mouth goeth a sharp sword, that with it he should smite the nations: and he shall rule them with a rod of iron: and he treadeth the wine press of the fierceness and wrath of Almighty God. And he hath on his vesture, and on his thigh a name written, KING OF KINGS, AND LORD OF LORDS." (Rev. 19:11-16)

As believers, one of our greatest hopes is knowing that Jesus IS coming back and we will spend eternity with Him. All our tears will be wiped away, there will be no more death, no more sorrow, and no more pain. We can only imagine.

3. "Thy Will Be Done in Earth as it is in Heaven."

Prayer is self-surrender! Not merely the surrender to the will of God of the thing for which we are praying, but deeper still—it means the surrender of the person who is praying to the will of God. It means a permanent surrender as a life attitude. There is a freedom in prayer that comes as a result of losing one's self unto the will of God. We must come to Him with this humble and perhaps, childlike attitude.

Three times in the Garden of Gethsemane, Jesus asks for "this cup" to be taken from Him and three times He says, yet not my will but Your will be done. When we surrender, we desire to do the will of God, we realize we are weak and surrendering ultimately brings *joy* to our hearts.

"And he went a little farther, and fell on his face, and prayed, saying, 'O my Father, if it is possible, let this cup pass from me: nevertheless not as I will, but as thou wilt'. And he cometh unto the disciples, and findeth them asleep, and saith unto Peter, 'What, could ye not watch with me one hour? Watch and pray, that ye enter not into temptation: the spirit indeed is willing, but the flesh is weak'. He went away a second time, and prayed, saying, 'O my Father, if this cup may not pass away from me, except I drink it, thy will be done'. And he came and found them asleep again: for their eyes were heavy. And he left them, and went away again, and prayed the third time, saying the same words." **(Matt. 26:39-44)**

God is in Heaven and Heaven is the home of God. It is uniquely His and though He is everywhere at all times, Heaven is the unmatched place of His residence and absolutely indescribable in human terms. Everything that is precious to us is in Heaven. Our Father is there, our Savior is there, our fellow saints of Old Testament and New Testament times are there, our name is there, our inheritance is there, our reward is there, our treasure is there, our citizenship is there. Heaven is our eternal home, and we're only aliens in this life.

"And I saw no temple therein: for the Lord God Almighty and the Lamb are the temple of it. And the city has no need of the sun, neither of the moon, to shine in it: for the glory of God did lighten it, and the Lamb is the light thereof. And the nations of them which are saved

shall walk in the light of it: and the kings of the earth do bring their glory and honour into it. And the gates of it shall not be shut at all by day: for there shall be no night there. And they shall bring the glory and honor of the nations into it." (Rev. 21:22-26)

The Bible also says the Holy Angels are there. In Isaiah 6, there is a picture of God high, lifted up, exalted on His Heavenly throne, and surrounding Him are the Holy Angels. In Luke 22:42-43, Jesus was in the Garden of Gethsemane, and said, *"Father, if thou be willing, remove this cup from me: nevertheless, not my will, but thine, be done. And there appeared an angel unto him from heaven, strengthening him."* Here we see a great example of the fact that Holy Angels come from Heaven and they also dwell in Heaven, the abode of God.

Jesus wants us to have true joy. The will of God is a joyous thing. People without Christ tend to think that happiness comes from things we pursue, buy or do, and this may be true in a shallow and very fleeting way. And, many people spend their entire lives chasing after these things. But true heartfelt and lasting joy is a gift from God to those who love Him. He ultimately wants all things to work for our good.

"And now come I to thee; and these things I speak in the world, that they might have my joy fulfilled in them- selves." (John 17:13)

"And we know that all things work together for good to them that love God, to them who are called according to his purpose." (Rom. 8:28)

Three Petitions Concerning Man and His Needs:

1. "Give Us This Day Our Daily Bread"

> *"God provides for His people. It is noteworthy that the request here is for daily bread, not daily steak or daily prime rib. God provides the necessities, but not always the niceties." (Sproul, R.C., 1984)*

When we pray this, we are asking God to give us that which sustains us for just one day. We are asking Him to provide for our physical, emotional and spiritual needs. We are trusting and have faith that He is going to provide for our future needs.

> *"We can be certain that God will give us the strength and resources we need to live through any situation in life that he ordains. The will of God will never take us where the grace of God cannot sustain us."* (Graham, B., 2017)

In the Sermon on the Mount, Jesus said,

> **"Therefore I say unto you, Take no thought for your life, what ye shall eat, or what ye shall drink; nor yet for your body, what ye shall put on. Is not the life more than meat, and the body than raiment? Behold, the fowls of the air: for they sow not, neither do they reap, nor gather into barns; yet your heavenly Father feedeth them. Are ye not much better than they?" (Matt. 6:25-27)**

*"Behold the
fowls of the
air; for they
sow not...yet
your Heavenly
Father fee-
deth them."*

By not trusting in His provision, we set ourselves up for anxiety, worry, and a grumbling unappreciative attitude. As in Numbers 11: 18-20, the Israelites were wandering in the desert, God miraculously provided them with bread in the form of manna. They began complaining and reminiscing about how good things were in Egypt, all the while, forgetting about the oppression, hardships and even torture they had endured at the hands of Pharaoh. So, when they cried out for meat, God told them you want meat, I'll give you meat, and you're going to eat meat until you're sick of it.

We must remember that in our fallen nature, we like to take credit for the sum of all our stuff, but God is the ultimate source of all our provisions.

> *"Every good gift and every perfect gift is from above,
> and cometh down from the Father of lights, with
> whom is no variableness, neither shadow of turning."
> (James 1:17)*

2. **"And Forgive Us Our Sins As We Forgive Those Who Sin Against Us"**

There Are Two Types of Forgiveness:

Judicial forgiveness:

Judicial forgiveness is granted by God because of the atonement of Christ. Judicial *forgiveness* is what God grants as Judge. It's the forgiveness God purchased for you by Christ's atonement for your sin. We receive judicial forgiveness when we believe and trust in Jesus as our Lord and Savior.

> *"For all have sinned, and come short of the glory of God; being justified freely by his grace through the redemption that is in Christ Jesus." (Rom. 3:23-24)*

This kind of forgiveness frees you from any threat of eternal condemnation. It is the forgiveness of justification. Such pardon is immediately complete, you'll never need to seek it again.

> Ephesians 1:7 says, *"In whom we have redemption through his blood, the forgiveness of sins, according to the riches of his grace."*

Judicial forgiveness deals with sin's *penalty*. *This* frees us from the condemnation of the righteous, omniscient *Judge* whom we have wronged. It provides an unshakeable *standing* before the throne of divine judgment.

Paternal forgiveness:

Paternal forgiveness is granted by God because we are His children.

The Story of the Prodigal Son – Luke 15:11-24

> In this story, a man's younger son asks for his portion of the inheritance, which he would normally receive at his father's death. Although the son was not entitled to any inheritance while his father still lived, the father graciously fulfilled his request. The younger son then leaves home and squanders his wealth away in "riotous living". Immature and rebellious, he wanted to be free to live as he pleased. But because of his poor choices, he's left in great need. So he hired himself out to a citizen of that country to feed pigs, the worst sort of degradation and humiliation imaginable for a Jew, as swine were the worst sort of unclean animals. Desperate, bankrupt, and hungry he had to hit rock bottom in order to come to his senses. When he realizes his mistake, he humbles himself and goes back to his father. He plans to beg that his father will take him back as a servant. Instead, his father welcomes him home as a son.

We are a part of God's family. . .we are His children. No matter what we do, He loves us and forgives us. This is not a free pass to do whatever we want but should instead be a great motivation to do what's right in every situation. When we do make bad choices, we are still part of God's family. Just like parents do not leave their children just because they do something wrong, God does not abandon us. When we realize our mistakes and ask for forgiveness, He is always ready to love us and welcome us home.

> *"Behold, what manner of love the Father hath bestowed upon us, that we should be called the sons of God: therefore, the world knoweth us not because it knew him not." (1 John 3:1)*

We all forget that we need to confess our sins on a *daily* basis. 1 John 1:9 says, *"If we confess our sins, he is faithful and just to forgive us our sins, and to cleanse us from all unrighteousness."*

Sometimes our sins are not apparent to us but we can ask God to reveal things in our lives that are not pleasing to Him, like listening to music that gratifies our sinful nature. Recently a Christian radio station had a challenge to listen for 30 days to see how it changed our relationship with Christ. I (Ronda) chose to listen only to the Christian station in my house and in my car and found that my thoughts became more positive and God centered.

Because we are in Christ we are regenerated and made new creatures (2 Cor. 5:17), but because we are in this world, we are defiled by it. In Psalm 139: 23-24, David says, *"Search me, O God, and know my heart: try me, and know my thoughts: And see if there be any wicked way in me, and lead me in the way everlasting."*

Just because we know that God is faithful and forgives us our sins, does not absolve us of our responsibility to confess our sins.

The channel of forgiveness is blocked as long as we do not forgive others. This is a tough one because we all have memories of people that have hurt us, who have said and done mean, thoughtless or hateful things. We'd rather pray that God send a lightning bolt their way. Perhaps we even find ourselves gloating or celebrating their ill circumstances and feeling justified in our attitude. *Before we bring our gifts to God, it is imperative that we first be reconciled to one another.*

> *"For if ye forgive men their trespasses, your heavenly Father will also forgive you: But if ye forgive not men their trespasses, neither will your Father forgive your trespasses." (Matt. 6:14-15)*

> *"Therefore if thou bring thy gift to the altar, and there rememberest that thy brother hath ought against thee; Leave there thy gift before the altar, and go thy way; first be reconciled to thy brother, and then come and offer thy gift." (Matt. 5:23-24)*

Our human nature wants vengeance but God's Word gives wise instruction as to how we are to respond to evil doers.

> Romans 12:17-21, *"Recompense to no man evil for evil. Provide things honest in the sight of all men. If it be possible, as much as lieth in you, live peaceably with all men. Dearly beloved, avenge not yourselves, but rather give place unto wrath: for it is written, Vengeance is mine; I will repay saith the Lord. Therefore if thine enemy hunger, feed him; if he thirst, give him drink: for in so doing thou shalt heap coals of fire on his head. Be not overcome of evil, but overcome evil with good."*

We are to repay evil with good!

"Not rendering evil for evil, or railing for railing: but contrariwise blessing; knowing that ye are thereunto called, that ye should inherit a blessing." (1 Pet. 3:9)

We are never more like Christ than when we extend forgiveness fully and freely to those who have sinned against us. Peter asked Jesus how many times do we need to forgive those who have sinned against us, seven times? Jesus said, ***I say not unto thee, Until seven times: but Until seventy times seven" (Matt. 18:22).*** What Jesus meant by this expression was that we ought to forgive others without limit. Why is this? The reason, Jesus went on to say, is because we should treat others the same way God has treated us. You see, we owe God a debt that is far greater than anything we could ever repay, a debt caused by our sin. But God in His grace has forgiven us anyway, not because we deserve it, but simply because of His love and mercy.

3. "Lead Us Not Into Temptation But Deliver Us From Evil"

Does this mean 'deliver us from evil' or 'deliver us from the evil one'? The Greek word for both is identical. In the context both make grammatical and theological sense.

'Evil' means *all* that is evil - whether evil actions, evil people or evil circumstances.

The *'evil one'* means the devil, who is the author of all evil actions, the prime mover of all evil people, and the instigator of evil circumstances.

He is the:

- Devil
- Satan
- Original tempter
- Original deceiver
- Great dragon
- Serpent
- Author of confusion
- Father of Lies
- The god of this world
- The Accuser

> *"And the great dragon was cast out, that old serpent, called the Devil and Satan, which deceiveth the whole world: he was cast out into the earth, and his angels were cast out with him." (Rev. 12:9)*

In Genesis 3:1-4, we see him as the serpent, who deceives Eve, enticing her to disobey God.

The evil one's deception is aimed to make us:

Worship false gods

Listen to and believe the messages, visions and dreams of false prophets

Be impacted by false miracles

Believe false christs

Believe lies

Believe sin is okay

Lead us away from God and the truth

HELLO GOD *it's Me*

In this prayer, Jesus is not suggesting that God will tempt us to do evil. God's word specifically states that God tempts no one.

> *"Let no man say when he is tempted, I am tempted of God: for God cannot be tempted with evil, neither tempteth he any man: But every man is tempted, when he is drawn away of his own lust, and enticed." (James 1:13)*

God may test, but He never tempts to do evil. A test is for growth, temptation is towards evil. The petition is not designed to avoid the trials of this world, but to protect us from vulnerable exposure to the attacks of Satan.

> *"I pray not that thou shouldest take them out of the world, but that thou shouldest keep them from the evil." (John 17:15)*

When we pray "deliver us from evil", we recognize Satan's power, affirm our weakness, and plead for the *greater* power of God! As believers in Christ and followers of Christ, we also recognize in Him we have His power!

> *"Ye are from God, little children, and have overcome them: because greater is he that is in you, than he that is in the world." (1 John 4:4)*

We also know what a wonderful privilege we obtain at the moment of salvation, and can trust in this amazing promise, telling us that we can approach God with boldness.

"Let us therefore come boldly unto the throne of grace, that we may obtain mercy and find grace to help in time of need." (Heb. 4:16)

When weak, tempted and in need of God's power - Pray this prayer:

Psalm 51- A Psalm of David

"Have mercy upon me, O God, according to thy lovingkindness: according unto the multitude of thy tender mercies blot out my transgressions.

Wash me thoroughly from mine iniquity, and cleanse me from my sin.

For I acknowledge my transgressions: and my sin is ever before me.

Against thee, thee only, have I sinned, and done this evil in thy sight: that thou mightest be justified when thou speakest, and be clear when thou judgest.

Behold, I was shapen in iniquity; and in sin did my mother conceive me.

Behold, thou desirest truth in the inward parts: and in the hidden part thou shalt make me to know wisdom.

Purge me with hyssop, and I shall be clean: wash me, and I shall be whiter than snow.

Make me to hear joy and gladness; that the bones which thou hast broken may rejoice.

Hide thy face from my sins, and blot out all mine iniquities.

Create in me a clean heart, O God; and renew a right spirit within me.

Cast me not away from thy presence; and take not thy holy spirit from me.

Restore unto me the joy of thy salvation; and uphold me with thy free spirit.

Then will I teach transgressors thy ways; and sinners shall be converted unto thee.

Deliver me from bloodguiltiness, O God, thou God of my salvation: and my tongue shall sing aloud of thy righteousness.

O Lord, open thou my lips; and my mouth shall shew forth thy praise.

For thou desirest not sacrifice; else would I give it: thou delightest not in burnt offering.

The sacrifices of God are a broken spirit: a broken and a contrite heart, O God, thou wilt not despise.

Do good in thy good pleasure unto Zion: build thou the walls of Jerusalem.

Then shalt thou be pleased with the sacrifices of righteousness, with burnt offering and whole burnt offering: then shall they offer bullocks upon thine altar." Amen

Chapter 3

WHEN OUR PRAYERS ARE HINDERED - A QUESTION OF FELLOWSHIP

What is Fellowship?

FELLOWSHIP IS A WORD USED IN CHRISTIAN CIRCLES A lot. It brings to mind several different images. To some "fellowship" represents potluck lunches or memories of summer camp as a youth. It may remind us of close friendships we enjoy or times shared in and around The Word. It is the bond that is created when people spend time together sharing commonalities.

Fellowship with God is impossible without a personal relationship with Jesus Christ. When we have a personal relationship with Christ, we become a child of God.

> *"But as many as received him, to them gave he power to become the sons of God, even to them that believe on his name." (John 1:12)*

We can call out to God if we have a personal relationship with Him and expect Him to respond. I can't walk up to a random stranger and say, "Will you make me lunch?" But I can go to my wife or husband and say, "Will you make me lunch?" I can ask that of them. And he or she can ask things of me as well. Those are the privileges of a personal relationship and fellowship.

The word fellowship in the New Testament is the Greek word *koinonia* (koin-o-nia) and usually conveys relationship, defined as, Fellowship, intimacy, communion, community, and/or partnership" (Strong, J., 1890). God desires to have fellowship with His children and we should desire fellowship with Him. In fact, God sent His apostles to preach the message of Christ so we could fellowship with Him. This relationship with God brings great "joy" *and* tremendous blessings accompany fellowship with Him!

Fellowship with God means Spiritual Communion

First, when we have fellowship with the Father, we have fellowship with the Son and all others who follow God. When we have fellowship with God we should never feel alone. There are many times when we *are* alone but God is always with us! When we were young, our parents used to sing the song, "In the Garden", and it is still a poignant reminder of this truth.

"In the Garden" is a gospel song written by American songwriter C. Austin Miles (1868–1946). According to Miles' great-granddaughter, the song was written "in a cold, dreary and leaky basement in Pitman, New Jersey that didn't even have a window in it let alone a view of a garden" (Wikipedia, 2020).

Lyrics:

I come to the garden alone,
While the dew is still on the roses;
And the voice I hear, falling on my ear,
The Son of God discloses.

Refrain: And He walks with me, and He talks with me,
And He tells me I am His own,
And the joy we share as we tarry there,
None other has ever known.

He speaks, and the sound of His voice
Is so sweet the birds hush their singing;
And the melody that He gave to me
Within my heart is ringing.

I'd stay in the garden with Him
Tho' the night around me be falling;
But He bids me go; thro' the voice of woe,
His voice to me is calling. (Miles, C.A., 1912)

Fellowship with God means Being Cleansed of Sins

Secondly, when we are in fellowship with our Father God, we have the benefit of continual cleansing of sin. As long as we are in a relationship with God, as His children we can constantly be made pure by the cleansing ability of Christ's blood. God cannot have fellowship with sin, He is light and in Him is no darkness.

Light is the absence of darkness, when we remain in the light (i.e. fellowship with God), darkness is removed and we are found pure.

> *"This then is the message which we have heard of him, and declare unto you, that God is light, and in him is no darkness at all. If we say that we have fellowship with him, and walk in darkness, we lie, and do not the truth: But if we walk in the light, as he is in the light, we have fellowship one with another, and the blood of Jesus Christ his Son cleanseth us from all sin."*
> *(1 John 1:5-7)*

Humanity does not acquire God's forgiveness through any technique like, meditation, or creative visualization. It is a free gift to be humbly received by faith and there is nothing we can do to earn it.

> *"For by grace are ye saved through faith; and that not of yourselves; it is the gift of God. Not of works, lest any man should boast." (Eph. 2:8-9)*

God extended grace toward Noah

God did not love Noah because he lived a godly life. Noah lived a godly life because he understood how much God loved him. There is a difference. The Bible says, *"we love him because he first loved us"* (1 John 4:19). God loves you and He loves me! Embrace that and be thankful for it – even when times are hard.

Great Blessings are Associated with Being "In Fellowship" with God

These blessings are wonderful representations of God's care and concern for His creation. However, they are conditional upon us maintaining real fellowship with God, His Son and His church. We cannot declare to have a relationship with God and still be living in darkness. First John 1:6-7 says, ***"God is light, and in him is no darkness at all."***

In 1 John Chapter 1 we see:

Jesus Christ - The Word of life, became flesh, giving us eternal life and making fellowship possible.

> *"That which was from the beginning, which we have heard, which we have seen with our eyes, which we have looked upon, and our hands have handled, of the Word of life; (For the life was manifested, and we have seen it, and bear witness, and shew unto you that eternal life, which was with the Father, and was man-ifested unto us;…)" (1 John 1:1-2)*

Our fellowship is with God the Father and God the Son and thus with one another making our joy complete as believers.

> *"That which we have seen and heard declare we unto you, that ye also may have fellowship with us: and truly our fellowship is with the Father, and with his*

Son Jesus Christ. And these things write we unto you, that your joy may be full." (1 John 1:3-4)

The Conditions of Fellowship

Walk in the light:

To walk in the light is to live in fellowship with God, with one another and to be purified from all sin. When Jesus was getting ready to leave this earth He told His disciples:... *"Yet a little while is the light with you. Walk while ye have the light, lest darkness come upon you: for he that walketh in darkness knoweth not wither he goeth. While ye have light, believe in the light, that ye may be children of light" (John 12:35-36a).* Choose to walk in the light or choose to walk in darkness. It's up to you. Walking in the light ensures the joy of our salvation and fellowship with other believers and with Him.

Agree with God about sin:

We have sinned; sin interrupts fellowship but confession restores that fellowship. We cannot have fellowship with God if we claim to be without sin. Immediate confession keeps the fellowship unbroken.

> *"If we say that we have no sin, we deceive ourselves, and the truth is not in us. If we confess our sins, he is faithful and just to forgive us our sins, and cleanse us from all unrighteousness. If we say that we have not sinned, we make him a liar, and his word is not in us."*
> *(1 John 1:8-10)*

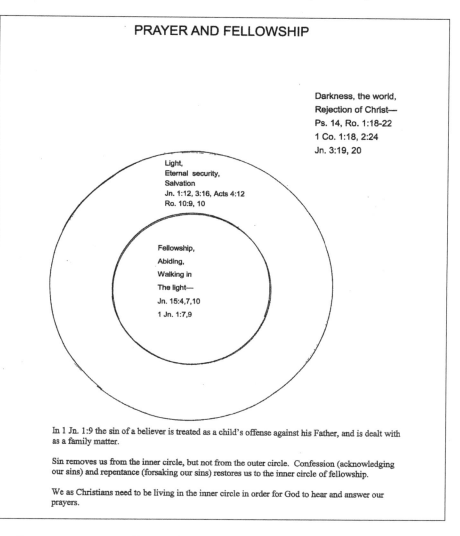

PRAYER AND FELLOWSHIP

Darkness, the world,
Rejection of Christ—
Ps. 14, Ro. 1:18-22
1 Co. 1:18, 2:24
Jn. 3:19, 20

Light,
Eternal security,
Salvation
Jn. 1:12, 3:16, Acts 4:12
Ro. 10:9, 10

Fellowship,
Abiding,
Walking in
The light—
Jn. 15:4,7,10
1 Jn. 1:7,9

In 1 Jn. 1:9 the sin of a believer is treated as a child's offense against his Father, and is dealt with as a family matter.

Sin removes us from the inner circle, but not from the outer circle. Confession (acknowledging our sins) and repentance (forsaking our sins) restores us to the inner circle of fellowship.

We as Christians need to be living in the inner circle in order for God to hear and answer our prayers.

Sin removes us from the inner circle but not from the outer circle. Confession (acknowledging our sins) and repentance (forsaking our sins) restores us to the inner circle of fellowship. In 1 John 1:9 the sin of a believer is treated as a child's offense against his Father, and is dealt with as a family member. We, as Christians, must be living in the inner circle in order for God to hear and answer our prayers.

*"If we confess our sins, he is faithful and just to forgive
us our sins, and to cleanse us from all unrighteousness."
(1 John 1:9)*

It's not just up to us to maintain this sweet fellowship. Thank
God! When Jesus was preparing to leave this world, He told His
disciples that He prayed to His Father and asked Him to give
another Comforter, the Holy Spirit, to abide with them forever,
dwell with them and be in them. They were saddened and afraid
that when Jesus left them physically, they would be without Him.
In His deep love for them (and all believers), He told them:

*"And I will pray the Father, and he shall give you
another Comforter, that he may abide with you for
ever... the Spirit of Truth." (John 14:16-17a)*

Jesus was getting ready to go to the cross, suffer and die for us.
*"And that he was buried, and that he rose again the third day according
to the scriptures" (1 Cor. 15:4).* So, we live in the hope of His return
someday to take us home to be with Him eternally as He said,

*"Ye have heard how I said unto you, I go away, and
come again unto you." (John 14:28a)*

And Jesus also said unto His disciples,

*"In my Father's house are many mansions: if it were
not so, I would have told you. I go to prepare a place
for you. And if I go and prepare a place for you, I will*

come again, and receive you unto myself; that where I am, there ye may be also." (John 14:2-3)

So, to maintain fellowship with God, we agree with Him about our daily sins, confess them and rest in the fact that there is *"...no condemnation to them which are in Christ Jesus, who walk not after the flesh, but after the Spirit" (Romans 8:1).*

Broken Fellowship

There are times and even seasons in our lives as believers, when we are not abiding with Christ and do not confess our sins daily, which is necessary to keep our fellowship with the Lord unbroken. Let's look at this example in John 13:1-11, where Jesus washes Peter's feet. It was just before the Passover Festival. Jesus knew that the hour had come for Him to leave this world and go to the Father... The evening meal was in progress...Jesus got up from the meal...and wrapped a towel around his waist..., poured water into a basin and began to wash his disciples' feet, drying them with the towel that was wrapped around him.

John 13:6-11, *"Then cometh he to Simon Peter: and Peter saith unto him, Lord, dost thou wash my feet? Jesus answered and said unto him, What I do thou knowest not now; but thou shalt know hereafter. Peter saith unto him, Thou shalt never wash my feet. Jesus answered him, If I wash thee not, thou hast no part with me. Simon Peter saith unto him, Lord, not my feet only, but also my hands and my head. Jesus saith to him,*

He that is washed needeth not save to wash his feet, but
is clean every whit: and ye are clean, but not all."

This is a wonderful example of how we need to daily wash our feet (confess and repent of our sins), even though our whole body is clean by the shed blood of Jesus Christ.

So, what about these times when our prayers are not effective, hindered and even, the Lord says, unheard? God's Word is clear on this matter:

When We Cherish/Regard Sin in our Hearts:

If you're practicing sin as a Christian, it will bring your prayer life to a screeching halt. Sometimes we say we have no sin because we see our own ways as the best or right way. It's our way or the highway. But our sins can separate us from God.

"But your iniquities have separated between you and
your God, and your sins have hidden his face from you,
that he will not hear." (Isa. 59:2)

When prayers are not answered, it is not because God cannot hear them. *"He that planted the ear, shall he not hear" (Psalm 94:9a)?* It may be that He simply refuses to hear. There may be other reasons, but we need to at least consider this possibility in any given situation of apparently unanswered prayer. Another possibility is for example James 4:3 which says, *"Ye ask, and receive not, because ye ask amiss, that ye may consume it upon your lusts."*

"Let the Spirit of God teach you what He is driving at and learn not to grieve Him. If we are abiding in Jesus Christ, we shall ask what He wants us to ask, whether we are conscious of doing so or not." (Chambers, O., 1989)

But perhaps Satan's most evil temptation is the pride of life, the very sin that resulted in his expulsion from heaven. He desired to be God, not to be a servant of God (Isa 14:12-15). Prideful boasting, which constitutes the pride of life, motivates the other two lusts (the lust of the flesh and the lust of the eyes, 1 John 2:16), and seeks to elevate itself above all others to fulfill all personal desires. It exalts the self in direct contradiction to Jesus' statement that those who would follow Him must take up their cross (an instrument of death) and deny themselves. The pride of life stands in our way if we truly seek to be servants of God. It comes not from the Father, but from the world.

Psalm 66:18 says, ***"If I regard iniquity in my heart, the Lord will not hear me."*** The Hebrew word meaning "to see" is raah: to see, see with accusative, look at, endure to see, absolute see (Strong, J., 1890). To regard or cherish sin in our lives means this: If I look at my life and *see* sin and nurture it (cherish), my prayers are futile. This is sin that is "held on to", "clung to".

There is a connection between practical righteousness and answered prayer - a connection made abundantly clear in Scripture. ***Proverbs 15:29 says, "The Lord is far from the wicked: but he heareth the prayer of the righteous."*** Even though as believers in Christ we possess a righteous standing before God based on Christ's work on the cross, and sin can no longer affect our judicial standing before God, our sin does affect our familial relationship. When we cherish sin in our hearts the ears of God may be closed to our prayers.

When We Cover Our Sins and Have Unconfessed Sin:

God instructs us not to rationalize, blame, or deceive ourselves in order to avoid confessing sin. We can't whitewash our sins and get by with it. We find mercy when we admit and turn away from our sin.

> *"He that covereth his sins shall not prosper: but whoso confesseth it and forsaketh them shall have mercy." (Prov. 28:13)*

> *"Behold, the Lord's hand is not shortened, that it cannot save; neither his ear heavy, that it cannot hear: But your iniquities have separated between you and your God, and your sins have hid his face from you, that he will not hear." (Isa. 59:1-2)*

In today's culture, we tend to look upon sin as something to be taken lightly. A little lie, a little cheating, so let's just ignore it, sweep it under the rug or laugh it off. But God looks at sin very seriously, so seriously that He sent His Son to die on the cross to pay the penalty for *our* sin.

> *Sin is a blasting presence and every fine power shrinks and withers in the destructive heat. Every Spiritual delicacy succumbs to its malignant touch. Sin impairs the sight and works toward blindness. Sin benumbs the hearing and tends to make us deaf. Sin perverts the taste, causing men to confound the sweet with the bitter and the bitter with the sweet. Sin hardens the touch and eventually renders one past feeling. All these are scriptural*

analogies and their common significance appears to be this; sin blocks and chokes the fine senses of the spirit and we become desensitized. (Jowett, J.H., 1863)

David was constantly confessing sin in the Psalms. We know that he is not saying that we must be holy in order to pray; otherwise no one would ever pray. In fact, being a sinner is one of the prerequisites for entering into the Kingdom of God. Jesus said that He did not come to call the righteous, but sinners to repentance (Luke 5:32). But confessing (acknowledging) and repenting (forsaking) our sin, and asking for forgiveness of our debts or trespasses, is an integral part of the practice of prayer. In fact, the more devoted we strive to be, the more painfully aware of our sin we will be.

King David confesses his sins, and acknowledges God's merciful forgiveness:

"When I kept silence, my bones waxed old through my roaring all the day long. For day and night thy hand was heavy upon me: my moisture is turned into the drought of summer. Selah. I acknowledged my sin unto thee, and mine iniquity have I not hid. I said, I will confess my transgressions unto the Lord; and thou forgavest the iniquity of my sin. Selah." (Ps. 32:3-5)

*Lord, thank you for these wonderful promises
that when I confess my sins and renounce them,
I find mercy. In Jesus Name, Amen.*

When We Have Idols in Our Hearts:

Have I made anything more important than God? God told Ezekiel…

> *"Son of man, these men have set up their idols in their heart, and put the stumblingblock of their iniquity before their face: should I be enquired of at all by them?"*
> *(Ezek. 14:3)*

In other words, God says, should I even let them pray to me? We estrange ourselves from God with idols in our hearts. Idols aren't always false images of God. *Anything* that becomes more important than our relationship with God is an idol - whether it's a person (even our mates and children), a social position, things, money, selfish ambition, habits that feed our pleasure, or even our reputation. What are your idols?

When We Make Meaningless Offerings Instead of Getting Right with God:

Our meaningless offerings can be things like doing good works, going to church, attending Bible studies, sacrificing our time and money, but unless we "put away" doing evil, God says He will not hear our prayers.

> Isaiah 1:14-16, *"Your new moons and your appointed feasts my soul hateth: they are a trouble unto me; I am weary to bear them. And when ye spread forth your hands, I will hide mine eyes from you: yea, when ye*

make many prayers, I will not hear: your hands are full of blood. Wash you, make you clean; put away the evil of your doings from before mine eyes; cease to do evil;..."

Proverbs 6:16-19 lists seven things which are evil and *abominations* to God:

> *"...A proud look, a lying tongue, hands that shed innocent blood, an heart that devises wicked imaginations, feet that be swift in running to mischief, a false witness that speaketh lies, and he that soweth discord among brethren."*

We need to be careful not to fall into the thinking that says, "I'm saved by God's grace, I'm covered by the blood of the Lamb, and I love God and others, so I can do whatever I want to do and I'm good with God." It is not enough, and is only part of the picture of our connection with Him. In 1 John 3:21b-22 it says, *"...we have confidence toward God, And whatsoever we ask, we receive of him, because we keep his commandments, and do those things that are pleasing in his sight."* This is the key of experiencing a prayer life that is effective!

Matthew Henry says about Judea and their sin:

> *Judea was desolate, and their cities burned. This awakened them to bring sacrifices and offerings, as if they would bribe God to remove the punishment, and give them leave to go on in their sin. Many who will readily part with their sacrifices, will not be persuaded to part with their*

*sins. They relied on the mere form as a service deserving a reward. The most costly lessons of wicked people, without thorough reformation of heart and life, cannot be acceptable to God. He not only did not accept them, but he abhorred them. All this shows that sin is very hateful to God. If we allow ourselves in secret sin, or forbidden indulgences; if we reject the salvation of Christ, our very prayers will become abomination. (*Henry, M., 1917*)

As believers our hope is *always* in the fact that when we draw near to God, He is merciful, full of grace and willing to forgive.

> **"For we have not an high priest which cannot be touched with the feeling of our infirmities; but was in all points tempted like as we are, yet without sin. Let us therefore come boldly unto the throne of grace, that we may obtain mercy, and find grace to help in time of need." (Heb. 4:15-16)**

When we do this, His eyes are open to us and His ears attentive to our prayers!

> **"If my people, which are called by my name, shall humble themselves, and pray, and seek my face, and turn from their wicked ways; then will I hear from heaven, and will forgive their sin, and will heal their land. Now mine eyes shall be open, and mine ears attent unto the prayer that is made in this place." (2 Chron. 7:14-15)**

Chapter 4

PRAYING IN THE SPIRIT

"You have a Father to pray to. You have a Savior to pray through. You have a Spirit to pray in. Let's be about our Father's business, praying in the Spirit." (Rogers, A., 1975)

What is Praying in the Spirit?

PRAYING IN THE SPIRIT IS A DIVINE GRACE GIVEN TO THE believer who has been placed into Christ upon salvation. It is a gift to the believer who chooses to walk in the Spirit, setting our minds on the things of the Spirit who leads us into truth. Scripture, the Word of God, is the main source of truth and is the Holy Spirit's weapon of choice - the sword!

> *"And take the helmet of salvation, and the sword of the Spirit, which is the word of God: Praying always with all prayer and supplication in the Spirit, and watching thereunto with all perseverance and supplication for all saints." (Eph. 6:17-18)*

"Take the Sword of the Spirit, which is the Word of God."

For us to "pray in the Spirit", it is essential that we remain surrendered because walking by/in the Spirit involves fellowship. As we learned in the last chapter, sin in our lives that we are knowingly and willingly clinging to, disrupts our relationship with our Lord. The good news is that if we confess our sins as believers and turn from our ways, God promises to forgive us.

Praying in the Spirit doesn't refer to the words we are saying. Rather, it refers to *the attitude of our heart*. Praying in the Spirit is praying in the power of the Spirit, by the leading of the Spirit and according to His will. It is praying for things the Spirit needs us to pray for and He prays for us when we don't know what or how to pray.

Romans 8:26 tells us, *"Likewise the Spirit also helpeth our infirmities: for we know not what we should pray for as we ought: but the Spirit itself maketh intercession for us with groanings which cannot be uttered."*

PRAYING IN THE SPIRIT

IS ⬍ IS

PRAYING IN THE WILL OF GOD

IS ⬍ IS

**BEING CONFORMED TO THE WILL OF GOD
AS WE PRAY**

IS ⬍ IS

SELF SURRENDER

IS ⬍ IS

ABIDING

(The arrows go both ways)

The greatest example in scripture of self-surrender and complete submission is our Lord Jesus in the Garden of Gethsemane.

Matthew 26:36-41, *"Then cometh Jesus with them unto a place called Gethsemane, and saith unto the disciples, Sit ye here, while I go and pray yonder. And he took with him Peter and the two sons of Zebedee, and began to be sorrowful and very heavy. Then saith he unto them, My soul is exceeding sorrowful, even unto death: tarry ye here, and watch with me. And he went a little farther, and fell on his face, and prayed, saying, O my Father, if it be possible, let this cup pass from me: nevertheless not as I will, but as thou wilt. And he cometh unto the disciples, and findeth them asleep, and saith unto Peter, What, could ye not watch with me one hour? Watch and pray, that ye enter not into temptation: the spirit indeed is willing, but the flesh is weak."*

Jesus prayed this same prayer to His Father, three times and He prayed till He sweat drops of blood. He knew what lie before Him and yet, He made the ultimate surrender. He surrendered to His Father's will, which was to suffer and die on the cross for our sins so we can have fellowship with Him and our scarlet sins become white as snow.

Jude 20, *"But ye, beloved, building up yourselves on your most holy faith, praying in the Holy Ghost."*

"Building your faith, praying in the Holy Spirit."

Isaiah 1:18 promises,

> *"Come now, and let us reason together, saith the LORD, though your sins be as scarlet, they shall be as white as snow; though they be red like crimson, they shall be as wool."*

The absolute yielding of the Son to do the Father's will, is the supreme example of the attitude we as children of God should have toward our Father.

Christ was:

Willing to go where His Father chose. He left heaven to come here.

Willing to be whatever His Father chose. He was willing to be spit upon and crucified.

Willing to do whatever His Father chose. He was obedient unto death.

At the end of John's first epistle, John tells us the key for God to hear and answer our prayers…. according to His will.

> *"And this is the confidence that we have in him, that, if we ask any thing according to his will, he heareth us: And if we know that he hears us, whatsoever we ask, we know that we have the petitions that we desired of him." (1 John 5:14–15)*

If we ask anything *according to His will*, He hears us - This is the proper and the necessary limitation in all prayer. God has not promised to grant anything that is contrary to His will, and it could not be right that He should do it. We should not wish to receive anything that is contrary to what He judges to be best.

Self-surrender = Abiding

A good definition of abiding is found in Galatians 2:20, *"I am crucified with Christ: nevertheless I live; yet not I, but Christ liveth in me: and the life which I now live in the flesh I live by the faith of the Son of God, who loved me, and gave himself for me."*

In the epistle of first John the phrase "abides in" is found 24 times, 17 times it refers to our abiding in God, and seven times to His abiding in us. The emphasis is on our abiding in Him. There is no question about His abiding in us if we will to abide in Him.

The great preacher, Charles Stanley says,

"I am the Light of the world:..."

"Abide in Him. You are a lousy producer. We all are. But as you abide in Him, the quality of fruit He will produce in your life will amaze you." (Stanley, C., 1995).

Jesus told His disciples, *"...I am the light of the world:..."(John 8:12)*; *"...I am the bread of life:..."*

(John 6:35); "...I am the Way:..." (John 14:6); and *"I am the Door:..." (John 10:9).* Now, the night before His death, He tells them, *"I am the true Vine:..." (John 15:1).* Like the other great "I am" passages recorded in the Gospel of John, it points to His deity. Each one is a metaphor that elevates Jesus to the level of Creator, Sustainer, Savior, and Lord—titles that can be claimed only by God.

> *"I am the true vine, and my Father is the husbandman. Every branch in me that beareth not fruit he taketh away: and every branch that beareth fruit, he purgeth it, that it may bring forth more fruit. Now ye are clean through the word which I have spoken unto you. Abide in me, and I in you, As the branch cannot bear fruit of itself, except it abide in the vine; no more can ye, except ye abide in me. I am the vine, ye are the branches: He that abideth in me, and I in him, the same bringeth forth much fruit: for without me ye can do nothing. If a man abide not in me, he is cast forth as a branch, and is withered; and men gather them, and cast them into the fire, and they are burned. If ye abide in me, and my words abide in you, ye shall ask what ye will, and it shall be done unto you. Herein is my Father glorified, that ye bear much fruit; so shall ye be my disciples." (John 15:1-8)*

The Vine, Branches and Fruit

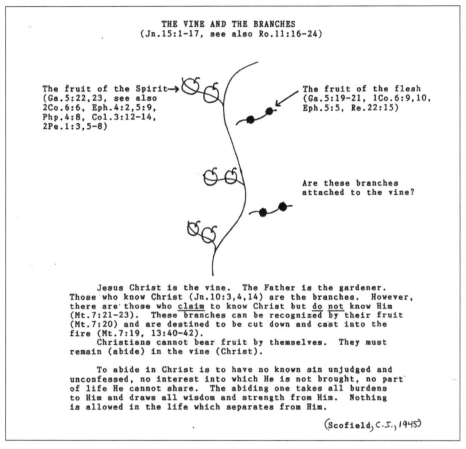

THE VINE AND THE BRANCHES
(Jn.15:1-17, see also Ro.11:16-24)

The fruit of the Spirit→
(Ga.5:22,23, see also
2Co.6:6, Eph.4:2,5:9,
Php.4:8, Col.3:12-14,
2Pe.1:3,5-8)

The fruit of the flesh
(Ga.5:19-21, 1Co.6:9,10,
Eph.5:5, Re.22:15)

Are these branches
attached to the vine?

Jesus Christ is the vine. The Father is the gardener. Those who know Christ (Jn.10:3,4,14) are the branches. However, there are those who <u>claim</u> to know Christ but <u>do not</u> know Him (Mt.7:21-23). These branches can be recognized by their fruit (Mt.7:20) and are destined to be cut down and cast into the fire (Mt.7:19, 13:40-42).

Christians cannot bear fruit by themselves. They must remain (abide) in the vine (Christ).

To abide in Christ is to have no known sin unjudged and unconfessed, no interest into which He is not brought, no part of life He cannot share. The abiding one takes all burdens to Him and draws all wisdom and strength from Him. Nothing is allowed in the life which separates from Him.

(Scofield, C.I., 1945)

Jesus Christ is the vine; the Father is the gardener, and those who know Christ are the branches. Christians cannot bear fruit in and of themselves, they must remain (abide) in the Vine (Jesus Christ). Abiding is when we are self-surrendered to the will of God and thereby produce good fruit by the Holy Spirit (Galatians 5:22-23).

"To abide in Christ is to have no known sin unjudged and unconfessed, no interest into which He is not brought, no

part of life He cannot share. The abiding one takes all burdens to Him and draws all wisdom and strength from Him. Nothing is allowed in the life which separates from Him." (Scofield, C.I., 1945)

Our responsibility is to bear the fruit the Holy Spirit produces through us. This is done by abiding in Christ through faith, Galatians 2:20: *"I am crucified with Christ: nevertheless I live; yet not I, but Christ liveth in me: and the life I now live in the flesh I live by the faith of the Son of God, who loved me, and gave himself for me."*

"The fruit of the Spirit is love, joy, peace..."

To abide in Christ is to draw upon His life. His life is made available through the presence of the Holy Spirit in our lives.

So, is abiding in Jesus something that is true of all believers?

There are certain Christian teachings that have made this unnecessarily complicated. They suggest that abiding in Christ is something additional, something special, that we gain through a crisis experience ushering us into a higher, deeper, or victorious life, sometimes even called the "abiding" life. And it is then suggested that Christians can be broken down into two groups: the "haves" and "have nots." The ordinary Christians who believe in Jesus but don't abide and the extraordinary Christians who believe and also abide.

But we think it's simpler and closer to the text to say that abiding, like faith itself, is a reality true of all Christians but also an experience that we grow into by degrees. It's not that some Christians abide and some don't. If you believe in Jesus, you are in Him. You are united to Him. You are connected to the life-giving vine. But no matter where you are on your spiritual journey, you can experience the reality of this connection to Jesus more and more.

You can become more fruitful. There are degrees of fruitfulness. The passage in John chapter 15, not only speaks of bearing fruit, but of bearing "more fruit" (v.2) and "much fruit" (v.8).

You can enjoy Jesus more. That's why Jesus says, *"These things have I spoken unto you, that my joy might remain in you, and that your joy might be full" (John 15:11).* He not only wants us to have joy, he wants us to have full joy.

And you can be more like Jesus. You can experience the sweetness, power, and joy of your connection to Him in greater degrees, as you grow in ongoing daily dependence on Him. In theological terms, all believers have *union* with Christ, but all believers can also have *communion* with Him in greater (or lesser) degrees.

To attempt to live the Christian life in the flesh is not merely difficult or simply a struggle. It's impossible. For apart from Christ we can do nothing. And none of us are righteous. But through faith in Him, God applies the righteousness of Christ to our account.

So how do we abide in Christ? By FAITH, Faith in the Son of God who loved us and gave Himself for us and BELIEVING that God will do as He has promised and walking in the truth of the Holy Spirit.

Who does the work?

God, through the Holy Spirit. God never intended His children to live defeated lives! The primary role of the Holy Spirit as leader and guide is to make us more Christlike in our character and behavior and to lead us down the path of righteousness. The idea is to walk in such a way as to avoid the moral landmines buried all around us. This is a positive approach. Instead of being told what not to do, we are given positive direction that will result in avoiding those things we have no business involving ourselves in. The Spirit life is not a life of DON'TS, it is a life of DO'S. *Do* walk in the Spirit and you will avoid fulfilling your sinful desires.

The power for effective prayer comes *not* from the state of *doing*, (do this, do that), but from a state of being *(be* conformed to the image of Christ).

To imagine yourself being happy or fulfilled with another person who is not your spouse, is to dwell on a lie. To envision yourself telling someone off and winning the respect of others in doing so, is to deceive yourself. To rehearse in your mind imaginary conversations in which you emotionally slam-dunk another person is to meditate on sin. To mentally devise a scheme where you are benefited at the expense at someone else is to fulfill the desires of the flesh.

So, what then is the standard by which we are to judge our thoughts?

"Finally, brethren, whatsoever things are true, whatsoever things are honest, whatsoever things are just, whatsoever things are pure, whatsoever things are lovely, whatsoever things are of good report; if there be any virtue, and if there be any praise, think on these things." (Phil. 4:8)

These are stiff criteria but this is war! Every day we engage in a battle to either walk with and abide in the Lord or walk in the flesh. Note the aggressive language in 2 Corinthians 10:3-5:

"For though we walk in the flesh, we do not war after the flesh: (For the weapons of our warfare are not carnal, but mighty through God to the pulling down of strong holds;) casting down imaginations and every high thing that exalteth itself against the knowledge of God, and bringing into captivity every thought to the obedience of Christ."

This is spiritual warfare at its most fundamental level. And to win the battle here (in the mind) is to eliminate dozens of potentials battles later on (in our behavior).

The Christian's most effective weapon for this battle is the *Word of God*. That is why Paul called the Word of God the Sword of the Spirit (Eph. 6:17). The Word of God is the weapon the Holy Spirit uses to expose and destroy the lies confronting the children of God. When we are confronted with evil, the weapon we are instructed to use is the SWORD, which is the Word of God!

John MacArthur teaches so well on this subject:

We want to be able to trust in this weapon. We want to know that if we're going to pick up the Word of God and use it that we're using the right instrument. If you, for example, question the inerrancy of Scripture, if you question the accuracy of Scripture, if you question the clarity of Scripture, if you question the integrity of Scripture, you're going to be reluctant to use it. If you equivocate on whether God wrote the Scripture, you're not going to be able to wield that. A high view of Scripture is necessary for the believer to be ready and eager to pick it up at every occasion... Our sword was not forged on human anvils or tempered in earthly fires. It is a weapon of divine origin provided for us by the Spirit of God to give us a powerful and effective instrument to use against everything that is raised up against the truth. That is why Christians need to hear, read, study, memorize and meditate on the Word of God on a daily basis.

If you're going to go forth into the kingdom of darkness and penetrate that darkness, you'd better know the truth of the Word of God so that you can defend yourself adequately against the deceptiveness of Satan. He's subtle. He's wily. He has very cleaver schemes...when you do come to know what Scripture teaches, you're like a spiritual young man who has overcome the evil one because you're strong in the Word and you've overcome the evil one...So if you don't know what Scripture teaches, you're highly vulnerable. And it's a sad thing that there are so many, many people so confused about things that are important, things that are issues of holiness, because they haven't searched the

Scriptures and come to know these things that are absolutely necessary. (MacArthur, J., 2020)

As believers, it is vital to our Spiritual health to be acutely aware of our Sword and its power. Hebrews 4:12 clearly states,

> *"For the word of God is quick, and powerful, and sharper than any twoedged sword, piercing even to the dividing asunder of soul and spirit, and of the joints and marrow, and is a discerner of the thoughts and intents of the heart."*

> *"So the Word comes, it saves. The Word comes, it establishes doctrinal truth. And then the Word cuts and breaks down and shatters the sinner (or the saint for that matter) that comes under its power. And then it picks the sinner (or the saint) back up in a restoring work to an upright position."* (MacArthur, J. 2020)

Praise God!!

The Holy Spirit is the person of God who walks with us, teaches us, convicts us and leads us into truth. As we yield to the Spirit, we are able to bear the fruit He produces.

> *"But the Fruit of the Spirit is love, joy, peace, longsuffering, gentleness, goodness, faith, Meekness, temperance: against such there is no law."* (Gal. 5:22-23)

When I (Rex), was going through all of the treatments for cancer, I became completely dependent on God. My life was in His hands. I was so weak that some days all I could do was pray silently to God. Even reading was too hard for me to do. In His mercy, God graciously removed my anxiety and replaced it with peace and even joy. It was simply amazing: the fruit of the Spirit was active and real.

The fruit of the Spirit is the most effective evangelistic tool we have. Why? Because unbelievers are not nearly as impressed with what we believe and preach as they are with how we act, especially under pressure. Our light is not primarily in the words we say, it is in the life we live.

In the back of my Bible, I (Ronda) have this quote by John MacArthur taped down:

> *"What's more, be aware that the world's eyes are upon you. They're looking for you to stumble and fall, but deep in their hearts, they're hoping you're for real. Because if you are that means there's a God up there – and there's hope for them too!"*

What a reassuring truth that one of the best ways to tell others about Jesus, is to live a life with our light shining!

Praying in the Spirit is our assurance as believers that we can stand in confidence that God hears our prayers and if we ask anything according to His will He hears us (1 John 5:14-15).

> *Rest assured that you can only succeed when you have laid your soul like a sheet of paper before the Lord, and asked him to write upon it; then it is no more your own prayer, but the Spirit making intercession in you according to the will of God. At a such time you need not say, "I hope God*

will answer the prayer; he will do it—he is pledged to do it. It is a kind of infidelity to say, "I do not know whether the Lord is true to his promise or not, but I hope he is." He is true; let God be true and every man a liar.... If the Spirit teaches you to pray, it is as certain as that twice two makes four, that God will give you what you are looking for. (Spurgeon, C.H., 1866)

Five Verses on Self Surrender

James 4:7

"Submit yourselves therefore to God. Resist the devil, and he will flee from you."

Romans 12:2

"And be not conformed to this world: but be ye transformed by the renewing of your mind, that ye may prove what is that good, and acceptable, and perfect, will of God."

Proverbs 23:26

"My son, give me thine heart, and let thine eyes observe my ways."

1 Peter 5:6-10

"Humble yourselves therefore, under the mighty hand of God, that he may exalt you in due time: Casting all your

care upon him; for he careth for you. Be sober, minded; be vigilant; because your adversary the devil, as roaring lion, walketh about, seeking whom he may devour. Whom resist stedfast in the faith, knowing that the same afflictions are accomplished in your brethren that are in the world. But the God of all grace, who hath called us unto his eternal glory by Christ Jesus, after that ye have suffered a while, make you perfect, stablish, strengthen, settle you."

Romans 12:1

"I BESEECH you therefore, brethren, by the mercies of God, that ye present your bodies a living sacrifice, holy, acceptable unto God, which is your reasonable service."

Chapter 5

THE PRAYER OF FAITH

"But without faith it is impossible to please him: for he that cometh to God must believe that he is, and that he is a rewarder of them that diligently seek him." *(Hebrews 11:6)*

In spite of the difficulties we encounter when we pray, prayer is a powerful and effective way to get right, stay right and stay free from error. "If any of you lack wisdom, let him ask of God, that giveth to all men liberally, and upbraideth not; and it shall be given him" (James 1:5). All things else being equal, the praying man is less likely to think wrong than the man who neglects to pray. "Men ought always to pray, and not to faint" (Luke 18:1). The apostle Paul calls faith a shield. The man of faith can walk at ease, protected by his simple confidence in God. God loves to be trusted, and He puts all heaven at the disposal of the trusting soul. But when we talk of faith let us know what we mean. Faith is not optimism, though it may breed optimism; it is not cheerfulness, though the man of faith is likely to be reasonably cheerful; it is not a vague sense of well-being or a tender appreciation for the beauty of human togetherness. Faith is confidence in God's self-revelation as found in the Holy Scriptures. (Tozer, A.W., 1964*)*

EVERY PERSON LIVES BY FAITH. WHEN WE SIT DOWN IN A chair, we trust that it will hold us up. When we put our money in the bank, we trust that it will be safe. When we drink a glass of water, we trust that it is not contaminated. When we go across a bridge, we trust it to support us. Life is a constant series of acts of faith. No human being could live a day without exercising faith.

The Prayer of Faith

Is Object Based:

For the believer, the object (like the chair) is God as He is revealed in the Scriptures. We trust and believe in God and that He will do just what He has said, holding fast to His Word, and in so doing, putting our hearts at peace. Faith doesn't create reality; faith responds to reality; the reality that God is who He says He is. It's not that you merely *believe* that counts, it's what or who you *believe in* that counts. You can choose to believe God, for He is Truth and Light.

What you choose to think is true, doesn't make it true. Jesus *did not* say "I am *a* truth, I am *one of many* truths". Today there is a widespread false narrative that says, "whatever you believe, that's true for you." Jesus shoots down this false thinking with a cruise missile because He said, *"...I am the truth"... (John 14:6)*.

And just before His crucifixion, Jesus said to Governor Pontius Pilate,

"...To this end was I born, and for this cause came I into the world, that I should bear witness unto the truth. Every one that is of the truth heareth my voice." (John 18:37)

Christ has endured once for all, and put away their sins for ever by the sacrifice of himself. Now this is the great object of faith. I pray you, do not make any mistake about this, for a mistake here will be dangerous, if not fatal. View Christ, by your faith, as being in his life, and death, and sufferings, and resurrection, the substitute for all whom his Father gave him, —the vicarious sacrifice for the sins of all those who will trust him with their souls. Christ, then, thus set forth, is the object of justifying faith. (Spurgeon, C.H., 1861)

The Psalmist writes *"...I trust in thy word" (Ps.119:42).*

"...And he shall direct thy paths."

King Solomon had God given wisdom and was the wisest man on the face of the earth in the Old Testament. Writing to his son, he warns him not to trust in his own wisdom but to *"Trust in the LORD with all thine heart; and lean not unto thine own understanding. In all thy ways acknowledge him and he shall direct thy paths" (Prov. 3:5-6).*

Are you able to say, from the relationship you have made with God, that He is a lovely Being? If not, ask God to bring you to this, so you may admire and experience His gentleness and kindness, that you may be able to say how good He is, and how delighted He is to do good to His children.

> Isaiah 46:4, *"And even to your old age I am he; and even to hoar* [gray] *hairs will I carry you: I have made, and I will bear; even I will carry, and deliver you."*

The Prayer of Faith

Is a Gift of Salvation:

The first act of faith in a believer's life is opening the door of our hearts to let Him in, trusting Him to be our Lord and Savior. In Revelation 3:20, Jesus says, *"Behold, I stand at the door, and knock: if any man hear my voice, and open the door, I will come in to him, and will sup with him, and he with me."* He will always be there for us no matter how far we wander away from Him and nothing can separate us from Him.

> *"For I am persuaded, that neither death, nor life, nor angels, nor principalities, nor powers, nor things present, nor things to come, Nor height, nor depth, nor any other creature, shall be able to separate us from*

the love of God, which is in Christ Jesus our Lord."
(Rom. 8:38-39)

Like the prodigal son, we can wander away from God and He will always welcome us back with open arms (Luke 15:11-32).

Salvation is both free and simple. Did you ever think about this? God had to make salvation free, otherwise poor people couldn't be saved. And God loves poor people just as much as He loves rich people. And God had to make salvation simple. Otherwise stupid people couldn't be saved. And God loves stupid people (like us) just as much as He loves smart people.

Paul tells us in 2 Corinthians 11:3, *"But I fear lest by any means, as the serpent beguiled Eve through his subtilty, so your minds should be corrupted from the simplicity that is in Christ."* Note that Paul emphasizes the simplicity of salvation.

Remember in Acts Chapter 16, when Paul and Silas were in jail, and God sent an earthquake and the doors flew open, and their chains fell off and the Philippian jailer comes running up to them and says, *"Sirs, what must I do to be saved?"* What did they tell him? They said, *"Believe on the Lord Jesus Christ, and thou shalt be saved..."* *(Acts 16:31).*

Salvation is free. Salvation is simple.

The Prayer of Faith

Is Unseen, Certain, Assured and Hopeful:

In Hebrews Chapter 11, the writer speaks of many of the Old Testament saints that God called upon to serve Him through faith, but they did not experience the full manifestation of God's promises in their life here on earth. They all died in faith, not having seen the promises (Heb. 11:13). They lived by faith, not by sight, knowing God always keeps His promises, no matter how long He takes to fulfill them. Each of us experience trying times when we can choose to either *"walk by faith, not by sight" (2 Cor. 5:7)*, or live in a state of anxiety and fear.

In 2 Corinthians 4:18, Paul tells us, *"While we look not at the things which are seen, but at the things which are not seen: for the things which are seen are temporal; but the things which are not seen are eternal."*

All too often, we act like our dogs, always sniffing and looking around for the next bush to pee on, instead of looking up toward the majesty and awesome power of God. If we do look to God, we just might hear Him saying, "Why are you wandering around in the bushes? Follow me."

The Prayer of Faith

Is Fruit of the Holy Spirit:

As we choose to obey, believe, abide and hold steady in our walk with the Lord, the Holy Spirit produces the fruit of faith and faithfulness in our lives.

> *"Put on therefore, as the elect of God, holy and beloved, bowels of mercies, kindness, humbleness of mind, meekness, longsuffering; Forbearing one another, and forgiving one another, if any man have a quarrel against any: even as Christ forgave you, so also do ye. And*

above all these things put on charity, which is the bond of perfectness." (Col. 3:12-14)

The Prayer of Faith

Is Exercised, Strengthened and Increased in Trials:

"My brethren, count it all joy when ye fall into divers temptations: knowing this, that the trying of your faith worketh patience. But let patience have her perfect work, that ye may be perfect and entire, wanting nothing." (James 1:2-4)

"Therefore being justified by faith, we have peace with God through our Lord Jesus Christ. By whom also we have access by faith into this grace wherein we stand, and rejoice in hope of the glory of God. And not only so, but we glory in tribulations also: knowing that tribulation worketh patience; and patience, experience; and experience hope: And hope maketh not ashamed; because the love of God is shed abroad in our hearts by the Holy Ghost which is given unto us." (Rom. 5:1-5)

"Throughout the Bible we find a simple formula: When the Word goes in, praise goes up, and faith goes out, God goes forth to strengthen His people."
(Jeremiah, D., 1994)

The Prayer of Faith

Is of the Righteous Man:

Our righteousness is obtained through our salvation and through our recognition of our human bankruptcy. God's ultimate goal is to make us like Christ (Rom. 8:29, I John 3:2). This does not mean we are "evolving" into godhood, as some religions teach. As we become more and more like Him, we discover our true selves, the persons we were created to be. God looks on the heart and it is more important that we are on our knees in our heart than on our knees literally.

> *"Confess your faults one to another, and pray one for another, that ye may be healed. The effectual fervent prayer of a righteous man availeth much. Elias was a man subject to like passions as we are, and he prayed earnestly that it might not rain: and it rained not on the earth by the space of three years and six months. And he prayed again, and the heaven gave rain, and the earth brought forth her fruit." (James 5:16-18)*

> *"Good works are important in the life of a believer, but they are a result of a grateful heart that is overflowing with thanksgiving and love for God. Work done with this motive will receive a reward."* (Scofield, C.I., 1945)

As Jesus was tempted by Satan in the desert, we know we also will be tempted. When we pray for God's intervention in our lives, we can rest assured that Jesus knows how it feels to be tempted. This provides assuredness that God hears our prayers and will help us.

"For we have not an high priest which cannot be touched with the feeling of our infirmities; but was in all points tempted like as we are, yet without sin. Let us therefore come boldly unto the throne of grace, that we may obtain mercy, and find grace to help in time of need." (Heb. 4:15-16)

We are:

Righteous by our Salvation in Jesus Christ

Judicial Justification – Based on Christ's completed work on the cross

Righteous by our Daily Sanctification

Parental Sanctification – Based on our daily walk
Righteous by the confession of our daily sins
Righteous by the submission of our will to His
Righteous by trusting in the Holy Spirit to intercede for us
Righteous by being humble and steadfast
Righteous when we pray with the right motives
Righteous when we pray with faith
Righteous when we pray with a spirit of forgiveness towards others
Righteous when we pray in Christ's name
Righteous when our heart is right with God
Righteous when we don't pray with selfish desires
Righteous when we don't reject God's call or ignore His advice
Righteous when we don't worship idols
Righteous when we don't turn a deaf ear to the poor

The Hebrews 11:1-39 passage is called "The Hall of Fame." It has been called "The Heroes of the Faith"; "The Honor Roll of Old Testament Saints"; "The Faith Chapter," and other things as well. What it presents to us is the power of faith, the excellency of faith; *it is faith in action.*

The 11th chapter is a moving account of Old Testament saints. They all attest to the value of living by faith, giving the examples of Abel, Enoch, Noah, Abraham, Sarah, Isaac, Jacob, Joseph, Moses, Rahab and others who kept their faith in the midst of trials and continued to be steadfast in their profession and belief in God.

The beginning point of faith is believing in God's character: **He is who He says He is and belief that Jesus is God is essential to salvation.** The end point is believing in God's promises: **He will do what He says.** When we believe that God will fulfill His promises even though we don't see those promises materializing yet, we demonstrate true faith!

So Biblical faith is sure and certain, *"the substance of things hoped for, the evidence of things not seen" (Heb. 11:1).*

Chapter Six

WAITING ON GOD - FAITH REST

We have been learning about, studying and practicing a more effective prayer life. Prayer is vital to the person who has put their faith in Jesus Christ as their Lord and Savior. It is the means by which we approach God the Father, through Jesus Christ.

We are reminded in Hebrews 4:16, *"Let us therefore come boldly unto the throne of grace, that we may obtain mercy, and find grace to help in time of need."* In this chapter, we are going to focus on the time in our life when we are praying and praying for something and we wonder if God even hears us. *(But now we know if we are in fellowship with Him, He does!)* We are waiting on God because there is something we believe we need, and we may even feel desperate. The majority of the time when we are waiting it is a *time of testing* our faith. We can choose to respond in the flesh, in our own ways, or we can choose to respond by applying the *Faith-Rest Technique.* We may be required to act or we may be required to be still in our thoughts and activities; but either way, the results depend upon God, not upon the seemingly clever actions we may take.

God Has a Plan

As we wait on God, we can enter a place of Divine rest. This is called *Faith-Rest*. It is our shelter in time of storm, it is our hiding place, it is our rock of solid foundation upon which we stand, it is our refuge, it is our peace, it is our strong tower, it is our green pasture, it is our still water, it is our peace which passes all understanding.

Waiting

Waiting for and on the Lord is referred to in both the Old and New Testament. The Old Testament is written in Hebrew and the New Testament in Greek. Following are the two definitions of the word "wait."

Hebrew definition of the word "Wait" or qavah (kaw-vaw):

> to bind together (perhaps by twisting), i.e. collect; (figuratively) to expect: gather (together), look, patiently, tarry, wait (for, on, upon). (Strong, J., 1890)

Greek definition of the word "Wait" or perimeno (peri-meno):

> remain, abide", remain all-around, i.e. *steady* (regardless of the obstacles involved); to "*endure*, putting up with *surrounding* difficulty." (Strong, J., 1890)

What is Faith-Rest?

R. B. Thieme, Jr. was the pastor of Berachah Church, a nondenominational Christian church in Houston, Texas, from 1950-2003. He developed the doctrine of Faith-Rest early on in his ministry. Many Bible teachers have since taught this principle.

Faith-Rest is taking a promise of God, a divine principle or a divine rationale, from God's Word, and placing our faith in that promise, principle or rationale. In order to enter into Faith-Rest: We must be in fellowship in order for the application of Faith-Rest to have any spiritual impact.

Since all men have faith, there is no merit in having faith. The merit is in the object of faith. We must place our faith in that which is true.

At salvation, we used an elementary form of Faith-Rest: we placed our faith in Jesus Christ.

In using the Faith-Rest technique, we may or may not act. The serenity prayer (later adopted by Alcoholics Anonymous) comes to mind: *"God grant us the serenity to accept the things we cannot change, the courage to change the things we can, and the wisdom to know the difference"* (Niebhur, R., 2020).

> *"The faith-rest drill is both a mechanic in the spiritual life and a means of growth. That is, God tests us with some pressure or difficulty, we apply the faith-rest technique (which may or may not require action), and we often experience some spiritual growth as a result."* (Theime, R.B., 1961)

We first heard of R.B. Theime when we were in our early teens. We have vivid memories of our mom working in the kitchen baking, cooking and ironing. On our kitchen counter sat a Wollensak Reel-to-Reel Tape Recorder, and almost every weekday afternoon while she worked, she listened to tapes of a Christian preacher by the name of Theime that she had ordered, after hearing him on the radio. His Texan accent resonated throughout the house as he taught a principle called *Faith-Rest*. Mom would say, *"You know God is not Santa Clause, there to give us whatever we want and ask for. He is there to give us stability and peace when we walk through tough times. He wants us to trust Him and believe His Word."*

For weeks on end, she listened to the tapes and we began to see a happier, less worrisome mother, with the ***"peace of God which passeth all understanding" (Phil. 4:7).*** So, when we began writing and teaching on having an effective and powerful prayer life, we sought out this teaching and technique, still believing and living by it with God's help. What a great Bible teacher Reverend Theime was!

Because Faith-Rest is such a difficult concept to communicate and understand, we need to reprogram our minds to a new type of reality. From physical birth, we have lived our whole life by a mental attitude called the "Human Viewpoint." To enter God's rest, we must learn to live by the "Divine Viewpoint." These two are opposite!

Human Viewpoint:

The human viewpoint looks at life through the limitations of human wisdom, strength and resources.

Divine Viewpoint:

The divine viewpoint looks at life through God's promise to work in us with His unlimited ability.

God has His plans for us that we may not be aware of. In our waiting we may move into the mindset of thinking God is gone away from us or He is angry at us or He doesn't care about us. But He knows we are waiting and in:

> Isaiah 55:8-9 He says, ***"For my thoughts are not your thoughts, neither your ways my ways, saith the Lord. For as the heavens are higher than the earth, so are my ways higher than your ways, and my thoughts than your thoughts."***

"As the Heavens are higher than the earth, so are my thoughts than your thoughts."

His plans are to work toward fulfilling His purposes for us. And they are good!

Romans 8:28 promises us that, *"...and we know that all things work together for good to them that love God, to them who are called according to his purpose."*

Nahum 1:7, *"The LORD is good, a strong hold in the day of trouble; and he knoweth them that trust in him."*

He already knows the plans He has for us and in spite of our human viewpoint, His plans are right, full of grace and in fulfillment of our greater purpose.

> *"For I know the thoughts that I think toward you, saith the LORD, thoughts of peace, and not of evil, to give you an expected end. Then shall ye call upon me, and ye shall go and pray unto me, and I will hearken unto you. And ye shall seek me, and find me, when ye shall search for me with all your heart." (Jer. 29:11)*

In this passage, the Israelites had been taken captive to Babylon because of their rebellion against God and God is promising that when they turn back to Him, He will bless them and restore them to their own land. He will put an end to their captivity, and turn away all their calamities.

Hal Lindsey describes Faith-Rest as:

> *"That principle taught in the Word of God by which we enter a divinely provided dynamic rest from struggling to live for God. This is done by believing the promises of God's*

Word, which releases God to work in and through us with His mighty power and wisdom." (Lindsey, H., 1986)

There are more than 7,000 promises (Korn, B., 2016) in the Bible to claim. As we lean on, and *believe* the scriptures, our attitudes and our minds are reprogrammed to the Divine Viewpoint.

Romans 10:17, *"So then faith cometh by hearing, and hearing by the word of God."*

However, it's not a name it and claim it kind of confidence. As faith comes by hearing, when we find ourselves struggling for faith, the best thing we can do is to get into the Word of God. This practically means getting your Bible out and reading or listening to it on a daily basis. The Bible is inspired (literally "God-breathed"), and it transforms our minds.

2 Timothy 3:16 says, *"All scripture is given by inspiration of God, and is profitable for doctrine, for reproof, for correction, for instruction in righteousness: That the man of God may be perfect, thoroughly furnished unto all good works."*

In Romans 12:2, Paul writes, *"And be not conformed to this world: but be ye transformed by the renewing of your mind, that ye may prove what is that good, and acceptable, and perfect, will of God."*

This is so powerful! Not only can we build our faith, but we can have our minds renewed; renewed by the Holy Spirit through God's Holy Word.

We then learn to *"walk by faith, not by sight" (2 Cor. 5:7)*, trusting only in God's promises. This new world of spiritual reality - the Divine Viewpoint, can only be found as we trust in God's Word. We then develop "Christ confidence" instead of self-confidence, as Paul did in:

> Philippians 4:13, *"I can do all things through Christ which strengtheneth me."*

The letter to the Hebrew Christians was written just before the destruction of the temple in 70 A.D. The Hebrew Christians were under persecution and were experiencing the danger of falling back into Judaism, and the writer is exhorting them to plunge forward into a *full* faith in Jesus Christ. In this text, Hebrews 3:7-4:11, the Lord deals with their wavering faith by giving both the sternest warnings and the greatest instruction and encouragement on how to enter His rest by faith in the face of trials and frightening times.

The Lord had brought the Hebrew Christians out of captivity in Egypt, through the Red Sea and into safety, wandering in the desert for 40 years. He wants them to enter the Promised land, Canaan. All but a couple were *still* not trusting and believing in God's promise. In Hebrews 3:10-12 the Lord says,

> *"Wherefore I was grieved with that generation, and said, They do always err in their heart; and they have not known my ways. So, I swear in my wrath, They shall not enter into my rest. Take heed, therefore*

brethren, lest there be in any of you an evil heart of unbelief in departing from the living God."

When we do not trust God, we grieve Him and we are not able to be at peace and rest in our faith.

The word *rest* is used 10 times in the passage. *Rest* in the future as a Heavenly *rest*, and *rest* emphasizing the present with the promise of the future. When Israel finally entered the promised land, they took possession of it by means of war. Though they ran after the enemy with drawn swords, inside themselves they were *resting* by faith in the promises of God.

This is the picture God draws to illustrate His *rest* and how to live the Christian life today. Though we are in the midst of a great spiritual war, we can *rest* inwardly and have perfect peace.

If we continually fail to believe God's promises, and instead worry and complain about life's circumstances, we are in danger of developing a pattern of unbelief that the Lord says is an "evil unbelieving heart that causes us to fall away from the living God (Hebrews 3:12). This is a description of the sin God considered the worst of all-failure to believe His promises. (Lindsey, H., 1986)

What We Can Do in Our Faith-Rest Waiting

Be in the Word:

As we fill our hearts and minds with God's Word, He can deliver us from worry and make our way prosperous and successful.

"This book of the law shall not depart out of thy mouth; but thou shalt meditate therein day and night, then thou mayest observe to do according to all that is written therein: for then thou shalt make thy way prosperous, and then thou shalt have good success." (Josh. 1:8)

"Be careful for nothing; but in every thing by prayer and supplication with thanksgiving, let your requests be made known unto God. And the peace of God, which passeth all understanding, shall keep your hearts and minds through Christ Jesus." (Phil. 4:6-7)

In a devotion titled, <u>Faith Over Feelings</u>, Pastor Greg Laurie (2019) says,

The Bible says the just will live by faith (see Romans 1:17). It does not say the just shall live by feelings. In fact, our feelings can mislead us. We can have all kinds of emotional reactions to all kinds of things...I think sometimes we come to church and want to have a breakthrough moment. We think we need an emotional touch. No, we don't. We just need to worship God whether we feel like it or not. We need to understand that the Christian life is a walk of faith...I think one of the best definitions of being a Christian is, to borrow Nietzsche's phrase, a "long obedience in the same direction." It's just putting one foot in front of the other and walking with the Lord every day. Some days you feel it. And some days you don't. (Laurie, G., 2019)

If we only believe what we feel, we will be led through life by one emotional impulse after another. When we begin by believing the truth of God's Word and walk by faith according to what we believe (God's Word), then our feelings will line up with what we think and how we behave. We can be guilty of what our dad referred to as "stinkin thinkin", a phrase that originated in AA (Alcoholics Anonymous), which is when we rely upon the shifting sand of our own selfish viewpoints and desires instead of relying upon the rock-solid promises of God's Word. There is an old hymn "Trust and Obey" which reminds us that trust, faith, and obedience go hand in hand. When we step out in faith, we must do so in the certainty of God's promises.

> *"But without faith it is impossible to please him: for he that cometh to God must believe that he is, and that he is a rewarder of them that diligently seek him."*
> *(Heb. 11:6)*

In Hebrews 12:1-3, the writer tells us we are to keep our eyes fixed on Jesus as we run our race of life with perseverance, throwing off sins that entangle us, and as we do so we will not grow weary or lose heart. We can depend on God's faithfulness while we are waiting on Him.

> *"He shall cover thee with his feathers, and under his wings shalt thou trust: his truth shall be thy shield and buckler." (Ps. 91:4)*

Be prayerful and persistent:

Prayer is one of the best ways to receive spiritual strength to wait. God is pleased when we don't give up praying and it is okay to be persistent in our prayer life. The root of our persistence is grounded in the realization we can do nothing without Christ. It is our utter helplessness that feeds our persistence.

In Luke 11:5-8, Jesus gives a great example of persistence in prayer. He tells his disciples, ***"...Which of you shall have a friend, and shall go unto him at midnight, and say unto him, 'Friend, lend me three loaves; For a friend of mine in his journey is come to me, and I have nothing to set before him? And he from within shall answer and say, Trouble me not: the door is now shut, and my children are with me in bed; I cannot rise and give thee. I say unto you, Though he will not rise and give him, because he is his friend, yet because of his importunity he will rise and give him as many as he needeth."***

Why did the man keep on knocking?
Because he had nothing!

Paul reiterates this in his letter to the Church at Ephesus when he writes, *"Praying always with all prayer and supplication in the Spirit, and watching thereunto with all perseverance and supplication for all saints" (Eph. 6:18).*

The Hunt for Gold

Years ago, Mr. Darby, a wealthy insurance broker from the East, was caught up with gold fever and headed out for Colorado. He did some prospecting and discovered a very rich vein of gold in the Rockies. He returned to the East and convinced all his friends to invest their money in the mining venture. They formed a corporation, bought a great deal of equipment, and mined his very wealthy vein of gold ore in Colorado.

About the time that the corporation paid off all its debts, the vein of gold ran out. The investors kept digging until they ran themselves into debt again. Finally, one day, a discouraged Mr. Darby ordered an end to the excavation. He closed the mine, went into Denver, and sold the mine and equipment to a junk dealer for a few hundred dollars. Mr. Darby headed back home.

The junk dealer hired a geologist to study the mine and the area. The geologist came back with a report; "if you'll dig three feet past the point of where Mr. Darby quit, you'll find that same vein of gold." The junk dealer became the wealthiest mine owner in the state of Colorado. Just three more feet! I wonder how many times, we too, stop three feet short of victory. (Smith, C., 1979)

Isaiah 40:31 (AMP), tells us, **"But those who wait for the LORD [who expect, look for, and hope in Him] Will gain new strength and renew their power; They will lift up their wings [and rise up close to God] like eagles [rising toward the sun]; They will run and not become weary, They will walk and not grow tired."**

Be still:

It is often difficult to be still and not try to rush God's plan in our life. But yet, when we choose to be still before God, the blessings are immeasurable. But, what does it mean to *be still? "Be still, and know that I am God" (Psalm 46:10).* This phrase is actually derived from the Hebrew word *rapha* which means "to be weak, to let go, to release" (Holmes, K., 2019). Essentially, it means *surrender. And know.*

In some instances, the word carries the idea of "to drop, be weak, or faint." Christians often interpret the command to "be still" as "to be quiet in God's presence."

While quietness is certainly helpful, the phrase means to stop frantic activity, to let down, and to be still. For God's people being "still" would involve looking to the Lord for their help. *"And Moses said unto the people, Fear ye not, stand still, and see the salvation of the LORD, which He will shew to you to day: for the Egyptians whom ye have seen to day, ye shall see them again no more for ever. The LORD shall fight for you, and ye shall hold your peace." (Exod. 14:13–14)*

In Psalm 46 we are instructed and encouraged as to how to respond when troubles come upon us.

> *"God is our refuge and strength, a very present help in trouble. Therefore will not we fear, though the earth be removed, and though the mountains be carried into the midst of the sea; though the waters thereof roar and be troubled, though the mountains shake with the swelling thereof, Selah. There is a river, the streams whereof shall make glad the city of God, the holy place of the tabernacles of the most High. God is in the midst of her; she shall not be moved: God shall help her, and*

that right early. The heathen raged, the kingdoms were moved: he uttered his voice, the earth melted. The LORD of hosts is with us; the God of Jacob is our refuge. Selah. Come, behold the works of the LORD, what desolations he hath made in the earth. He maketh wars to cease unto the end of the earth; he breaketh the bow, and cutteth the spear in sunder; he burneth the chariot in the fire. 'Be still, and know that I am God; I will be exalted among the heathen, I will be exalted in the earth.' The LORD of hosts is with us; the God of Jacob is our refuge. Selah"

Be assured:

As children of God, we are His sheep and He is our Shepherd. We hear His voice and we can never be snatched out of His hand. He will never leave us or forsake us!

Romans 8:37-39, *"Nay, in all these things we are more than conquerors through him that loved us. For I am persuaded, that neither death, nor life, nor angels, nor principalities, nor powers, nor things present, nor things to come, Nor height, nor depth, nor any other creature, shall be able to separate us from the love of God, which is in Christ Jesus our LORD."*

Psalm 23:2, *"He maketh me to lie down in green pastures..."*

John 10:27-28, *"My sheep hear my voice, and I know them, and they follow me: And I give unto them eternal life; and they shall never perish, neither shall any man pluck them out of my hand."*

Hebrews 13:5, *"...I will never leave thee nor forsake thee."*

Be wise:

When we are waiting, our *human* nature and *human* viewpoint often causes impatience, leading us to make foolish choices, or snap decisions lacking wisdom. This can lead us down a self-destructive path. God tells us if we are lacking wisdom to ask *Him* and He will give it to all men liberally (James 1:5). We are to seek Godly counsel. In 1 Kings 12:8 Solomon's son, Rehoboam, abandoned and forsook his father's wise ways and the counsel of the wise elders his father had given to him. He foolishly consulted the young men he had grown up with and therefore promised the people of Israel that the yoke of taxes and hard labor his father had placed upon them, he would make even heavier, thereby splitting the kingdom of Israel. He did not look to God either.

When we become a child of God (John 1:12), we need to look toward God and His Holy Word for wisdom rather than toward the *"philosophy and vain deceit after the tradition of men" (Col. 2:8)*. When we are waiting for God to speak to us, we need to remember our FAITH. Faith is trusting God in spite of how things look to us and in spite of our circumstances.

Psalm 40:1-3, is a Psalm of David to the chief Musician and says:

"I waited patiently for the LORD; and he inclined unto me, and heard my cry. He brought me up also out of an horrible pit, out of the miry clay, and set my feet upon a rock, and established my goings. And he hath put a new song in my mouth, even praise unto our God: many shall see it, and fear, and shall trust in the LORD."

So, to be wise while waiting, we must first look to God's Word, seek counsel from those who are walking with the Lord, such as our pastor and Christians who are steeped in God's Word. We must be careful not to make decisions based on our own perception or interpretation. He has our back!

Be singing and praising:

A Christian is a person who believes and trusts in God's promises. Sing and make music from your heart, always giving thanks to God.

All told, the Bible contains over four hundred references to singing and fifty direct commands to sing. The longest book of the Bible, the Psalms, is a book of songs. And in the New Testament we're commanded to sing psalms, hymns, and spiritual songs to one another.

Ephesians 5:19-20 says, *"Speaking to yourselves in psalms and hymns, and spiritual songs, singing and making melody in your heart to the LORD; Giving thanks always for all things unto God and the Father in the name of our Lord Jesus Christ."*

And Colossians 3:16 says, *"Let the word of Christ dwell in you richly in all wisdom; teaching and admonishing one another in psalms and hymns and spiritual songs, singing with grace in your hearts to the Lord."*

Why is it so important to sing unto the Lord?

Why does God so often tell us not simply to praise Him but to *sing* His praises? Why not just pray and read God's Word? Why sing? Why are God's people throughout history always singing? Why words *and* music and not just words alone? Why does God want us to sing?

One reason is that God Himself sings.

Zephaniah 3:17 says, *"... he will rejoice over thee with joy; he will rest in his love, he will joy over thee with singing."*

On the eve of His crucifixion, Jesus sang a hymn with His disciples (Matt. 26:30). He knows He is awaiting crucifixion for the sins of the world and He sings with His disciples! When we are in a trial and feeling saddened, overwhelmed, tired/weak, burned out, depressed, insecure, and alone we just don't feel like singing. Turning to the Psalms can move our hearts to sing. God's heart for setting words to melodies is evident from even a casual reading of the Psalms.

"Oh, sing unto the LORD a new song: sing unto the LORD, all the earth. Sing unto the LORD, bless

his name; shew forth his salvation from day to day."
(Ps. 96:1-2)

"Sing praises to God; sing praises: sing praises unto our
King, sing praises." (Ps. 47:6)

In just three verses we're commanded to sing *seven* times.

Music is powerful and has visible effects on the brain. We are to praise God in all circumstances, our storms, remembering His eye is on the sparrow and we know He is watching over us, and we are reminded of His faithfulness. We encourage you to find a Christian radio station you like and spend some time each day listening and singing along out loud or in your heart.

"We worship a triune God who sings, and he wants us to
be like him." (Piper & Taylor, 2009)

Music based on Scripture is very edifying and uplifting. Matt Redman's song, "10,000 Reasons (Bless the Lord)"perfectly suits Redman's paraphrase of Psalm 103, and the chorus will be singing in your head the rest of the day.

The song begins with the chorus, a paraphrase of the beginning of Psalm 103:

"Bless the Lord, O my soul
O my soul
Worship His holy Name
Sing like never before
O my soul"

Singing to the Lord is an act of worship and it is a way to pray when words cannot express.

Be serving:

A wonderful way to wait is to "busy" ourselves by serving others. This allows us to gain and maintain our "Heavenly" perspective and greater peace as we use the gifts God has given us. Our focus is taken off of ourselves and put on others.

A prime example was given by Jesus after the last supper when He washed His disciple's feet. He says to them,

> *"Know ye what I have done to you? Ye call me Master and Lord: and ye say well; for so I am. If I then, your Lord and Master, have washed your feet; ye also ought to wash one another's feet. For I have given you an example, that ye should do as I have done to you." (John 13:12b-14)*

One of the things Jesus was teaching was that we should serve others. If Jesus, who is Lord of all, would choose to lower Himself to do the job of the least important servant by washing His friends' feet, then we should always be willing to serve others. Jesus said to follow His example. Foot washing was very common in Bible times, but not very common today.

There are times we are called to do things for people that are without much hope. In Matthew 25:44-45, Jesus is telling a story in His discourse on the Mount of Olives about the treatment of those who are in need:

"...Lord, when saw we thee an hungred, or athirst, or a stranger, or naked, or sick, or in prison, and did not minister unto thee? Then shall he answer them, saying, Verily I say unto you, Inasmuch as ye did not to one of the least of these, ye did it not to me."

In other words, Jesus is saying, if you are not serving others as you are called to, you are not serving Me.

In the following passage, Paul tells us to have the mind of Christ, rejoicing in lowly service.

"Let nothing be done through strife or vainglory; but in lowliness of mind let each esteem other better than themselves. Look not every man on his own things, but every man also on the things of others. Let this mind be in you, which was also in Christ Jesus; Who being in the form of God, thought it not robbery to be equal with God: But made himself of no reputation and took upon him the form of a servant, and was made in the like-ness of men." (Phil. 2:3-7)

"He makes me lie down in green pastures..."

When we put others before ourselves, serving them and not looking to our own interests, waiting for God to answer our prayers becomes secondary in our daily lives. And in the process, we are blessed. Some examples of serving others can be cooking a meal, helping people move, praying with those in need, or running errands for those who are homebound. Each of us have something we can do for another.

Ask yourself, "what is something you might do to serve another person today?" Listen for answers.

Be faithful:

It is crucial to be faithful to the Lord during a time of testing. By choosing to remain faithful to God and His commands during your period of waiting, you receive even more power from the Holy Spirit and more endurance to press on in faith and not give up.

> *"Wherefore seeing we also are compassed about with so great a cloud of witnesses, let us lay aside every weight, and the sin which doth so easily beset us, and let us run with patience the race that is set before us. Looking unto Jesus the author and finisher of our faith: who for the joy that was set before him endured the cross, despising the shame, and is set down at the right hand of the throne of God." (Heb. 12:1-2)*

When we do *not* choose to walk in obedience to God and his commands, we grieve the Holy Spirit and hinder God's ability to guide and direct our path. We can suffer great consequences when we lean on our own earthly knowledge and experience. When we trust God with all of our heart and do not rely on our perception or understanding of the situation we are in, the path before us is made straight. God produces the fruit of the Holy Spirit in our lives when we are walking in obedience to Him.

> *"And Samuel said, Hath the LORD as great delight in burnt offerings and sacrifices, as in obeying the voice of the LORD? Behold, to obey is better than sacrifice, and to hearken than the fat of rams." (1 Sam. 15:22)*

Be expectant:

Wait upon the Lord with great expectation. Believe He has a wonderful plan for your future and He is able to bring it to pass in His perfect time.

God reigns and rules over every aspect of our lives. Nothing is an accident, nor can anything happen to you that He has not ordained. Sickness, tragedy, pain, or want will never strike without His permission. Everything has a purpose that will result in His glory and our good.

> *"And the LORD, he it is that doth go before thee; he will be with thee, he will not fail thee; neither forsake thee: fear not, neither be dismayed." (Deut. 31:8)*

All of His plans for us are good!

> Jeremiah 29:11-13 says, *"For I know the thoughts that I think toward you, sayeth the LORD, thoughts of peace, and not of evil, to give you an expected end. Then shall ye call upon me and ye shall go and pray unto me, and*

I will hearken unto you. And ye shall seek me, and find me, when ye shall search for me with all your heart."

We know God *"…is able also to save them to the uttermost that come unto God by him" (Heb. 7:25)* and *"…able to keep you from falling, and to present you faultless before the presence of his glory with exceeding joy" (Jude 24).*

There are 17 things listed in Romans 8 which can never separate us from the love of Christ:

- Tribulation
- Distress
- Persecution
- Famine
- Nakedness
- Peril
- Sword
- Death
- Life
- Angels
- Principalities
- Powers
- Things present
- Things to come
- Height
- Depth
- Any other creature

When we earnestly seek God through Bible study and prayer, then He will be *"...a lamp unto my feet, and a light unto my path"* *(Ps. 119:105).*

Be thankful:

No matter what you are waiting on God to do in your life, you can *choose* to be thankful. Giving thanks changes our perspective and makes our journey far more joyful than being anxious and stressed out over the details and timing. God has our situation under control!

> *"Rejoice evermore. Pray without ceasing. In every thing give thanks: for this is the will of God in Christ Jesus concerning you." (1 Thess. 5:16-18)*

At our age we wake up and say "thank you Lord for another day". Count your blessings and name them out loud. It can be as simple as thanking Him for a bed to sleep in, food to eat, and a roof over our head.

> *"The LORD is good unto them that wait for him, to the soul that seeketh him. It is good that a man should both hope and quietly wait for the salvation of the LORD." (Lam 3:25-26)*

> *"Wait on the LORD: be of good courage, and he shall strengthen thine heart: wait, I say, on the LORD." (Ps. 27:14)*

The Lord has strewn the pages of God's Word with promises of blessedness to those who wait for Him. And remember, His slightest Word stands fast and sure; it can never fail you. So, my soul, see that you have a promise underneath thee, for then your waiting will be resting and a firm foothold for your hope will give you confidence in Him who has said, "They shall not be ashamed that wait for Me" (Psalm 25:3a). (Spurgeon, S., 2006)

Verses About Waiting on the Lord

Hosea 12:6*:* ***"Therefore turn thou to thy God: keep mercy and judgement, and wait on thy God continually."***

Psalm 33:20*:* ***"Our soul waiteth for the LORD: he is our help and our shield."***

Psalm 130:5*:* ***"I wait for the LORD, my soul doth wait, and in his word do I hope."***

Isaiah 40:31*:* ***"But they that wait upon the LORD shall renew their strength; they shall mount up with wings as eagles, they shall run, and not be weary; they shall walk, and not faint."***

Psalm 37:7*:* ***"Rest in the LORD, and wait patiently for him: fret not thyself because of him who prospereth in his way, because of the man who bringeth wicked devices to pass."***

Psalm 40:1-3*: "I WAITED patiently for the LORD; and he inclined unto me, and heard my cry. He brought me up also out of an horrible pit, out of the miry clay, and set my feet upon a rock, and established my goings. And he hath put a new song in my mouth, even praise unto our God: many shall see it, and hear, and shall trust in the LORD."*

The verses above speak volumes about waiting for and upon Him. Here are some of the benefits of waiting.

We observe His kindness and justice

We are commanded to be strong and let our heart take courage

We are blessed for remaining steadfast

We reflect upon how He has been merciful and compassionate to His children

The Lord waits so He may be gracious to us

The Lord waits so He may be exalted

The Lord waits so He may have mercy upon us

In waiting we realize the Lord is a God of justice

Blessed are all who wait for Him

As we wait, we come to know He is our help and our shield

As we wait, in His word we do hope

As we wait, we will renew our strength

As we wait, we will mount up with wings as eagles

As we wait, we will run and not be weary

As we wait, we will walk and not faint

In waiting we are to be still before the Lord

As we wait, we are not to fret over those who prosper

As we wait, we are not to fret over the evil doers

We are to wait patiently for Him

As we wait patiently, He inclines to us and hears our cries

He draws us up from a pit of destruction

He sets our feet upon a rock

He makes our steps secure

He puts a new song, a song of praise in my mouth

Many will see and fear and put their trust in the Lord

Blessed is the one who puts his trust in the Lord

He multiplies His wonderous thoughts and deeds towards us

We proclaim of the mighty things He has done for us

The reason we wrote this book is not only to serve as a simple guide for communicating with God, but also to encourage you to believe in the rock-solid promises of God. Biblical faith is a sure thing, ***"the substance of things hoped for, the evidence of things not seen" (Heb. 11:1).***

"Faith is the substance of things hoped for..."

When God says something, you can take it to the bank and cash it. Our security is present possession, but it lasts for eternity. That's a long time. Speaking of those who believe in Him, Jesus said, *"And I give unto them eternal life; and they shall never perish, neither shall any man* [or anyone, including Satan] *pluck them out of my hand" (John 10:28).*

Someday Jesus is coming back, and He will take His children to Heaven with Him. If you have *not* put your faith and trust in Jesus as your Lord and Savior, then you are *not* one of His children, and your eternal destiny is with the devil and his angels, not Heaven.

Here is a simple prayer of salvation:

"Dear Jesus, thank you for dying on the cross for my sins and rising from the dead, giving me eternal life. I open the door of my heart to personally receive You as my Lord and Savior. Take control of my life and help me become the person You created me to be. In Jesus Name. Amen."

It is our prayer that this book will lead to a real relationship with King Jesus.

"The real purpose of prayer is to see the work of God accomplished in my life and then, through my life, in the lives of others." (Smith, C., 1984)

Appendix

KEEPING A PRAYER JOURNAL

THERE ARE MANY GREAT REASONS TO KEEP A PRAYER journal. Pick out a special notebook for your journal, one that beckons you! Some Christians keep a journal of a particular time or struggle in their lives and daily prayers that were prayed along with the answered prayers, while others keep a daily prayer journal, weekly, or from time to time. Some families keep a prayer journal on their kitchen table and each family member can write down their prayer requests for family prayer time. What a faith builder!

There are never any dumb prayers to God. He loves the fact that His child is taking time to spend with Him, seek Him and call to Him. Remember, you can pray anywhere! When you're driving (but keep your eyes open!), taking a walk or as a part of your quiet times, day or night. Some like to speak their prayers out loud. In whatever way you choose to keep a prayer journal, keep one!

We are quick to ask, plead, beg and argue with God about our problems, big or small but we are amazingly forgetful when He answers our prayers. By writing down your thoughts, prayers, praises and thanks, and writing down the answers, you have a perfect reminder of how He listened to and answered your prayers.

When you ask others to pray for and with you, be sure to share your answered prayers with them. We are told to bear one another's burdens (Gal. 6:2) and to encourage one another (1 Thess. 5:11).

My dear friend Sue, shares her love for keeping a prayer journal and says,

> *I started journaling prayers when my daughter was young. I did it mainly because my mind wanders when I pray, especially when I am tired. Writing my prayers to God was just Him and me sitting there talking and I was telling Him all my stuff. I just write all the things I am concerned about, just like I had my best friend who loves me and wants to know what is going on in my life. The only thing, He is the King of the universe and He can help with any problem that comes up. He has all the answers for all my dilemmas. Sometimes I include scriptures I am memorizing. This helps me with the memorization, plus it helps me with the answers because He talks to me through His Word. I may also include things I have heard preachers and teachers say that day, or things I have read in a Christian book I don't want to forget. The main reason I started writing my prayers is for my children, and I have told my friends when I die, I want my children to read my prayer journals and see how I prayed for them, and what God has done. Over all, this is one of the best things that I have done. It has brought me joy, comfort and peace of mind. I also write out praises to God. That is one of the most important parts of the journaling. Remembering who is there with you. Try it, I think you will like it.*

For over 30 years, I (Ronda) have been blessed to be in a group of Godly Christian women who are committed to meeting together to pray for each other. We meet a couple times each month in a home of one of the members. We take turns and keep it simple. Around noon we meet and visit for a half hour with snacks prepared by the hostess. Each person writes down their requests on a notecard and then we take another person's card, sit down and pray around the circle. It is our habit to begin our prayers with worshipping our Lord, thanking Him and praising Him for who He is and what He's done in our lives. Then, we pray for the requests written down on the card of the person we are praying for. Sometimes, all that is on the card is praise for all God's goodness and thanksgiving for answered prayer. As we go around the circle, often we are tearfully asking God to forgive us of our failings, hear our prayers, praising and thanking Him. At the end of our prayer time, we dismiss.

This has been one of the most important, meaningful and encouraging events in my walk as a believer. I cannot tell you how many times I have struggled to get to this time with my sisters and arrived in a state of frustration, sadness or anger. I have always left with a renewed spirit, hope and joy. James 5:16 says, *"Confess your faults one to another, and pray one for another, that ye may be healed. The effectual fervent prayer of a righteous man availeth much."* Over the last 30+ years, we have witnessed countless answers and even miracles to our prayers! God is so faithful.

Looking back at the way God has worked things out in our lives is one wonderful way to learn to trust God. As we read of His interventions over and over, we are then encouraged to draw closer to Him, putting our life under His gaze.

I (Ronda) remember a vivid illustration of trusting God on the front cover of a monthly magazine from a popular Christian organization. The picture was of a little girl, jumping off the edge of a swimming pool into the arms of her daddy. When we pray, we are putting our life in His hands, trusting He will take care of us. I often reflect on this pictorial representation, take a deep breath and jump off the edge into my Heavenly Father's arms.

Keeping a Prayer Journal

- Increases our faith
- Helps us focus attention on our prayer time
- Encourages us to pray every day
- Organizes our prayer life
- Shows us that God answers prayer
- Reminds us of God's faithfulness

Suggested Weekly Prayers

Sunday: Our church, missionaries, Christian missions in all parts of the world

Monday: Pastors, evangelists, Christian administrators and teachers

Tuesday: Churches, Christian schools, Christian businesses and Christian causes

Wednesday: Saved relatives, saved friends, Sunday school department and class members, home Bible study groups and members

Thursday: Special/personal list of the Lost

Friday: Political leaders, our government, our country, Israel

Saturday: Things pertaining directly to myself and my family

> *Prayer is not something we engage in because we wish to achieve anything. Prayer is communion with God. It is the act of being with Him and nothing more, nothing less. Now a great many things come of this later on, when you've been at it awhile. But in the beginning, that's all it is – being with God. You don't pray in order to achieve something. You pray in order to be with God.* (Killinger, J., 2012)

FIFTY PRAISE AND WORSHIP SONGS

A Poll

"SINGING IS PRAYING TWICE" IS A PHRASE WE OFTEN HEAR.
It's true when we sing to the Lord we enter into His courts. We
took a poll of many of our close friends and family, asking them
to share their favorite hymns, praise and worship song(s). Many
responded with comments as to why they chose their song(s) and
we are sharing these anonymous comments with you!

The following is some of the comments, songs and videos on
YouTube. We hope this is an extra blessing for each of you and adds
a deeper dimension of expression to your prayer time.

Prayer Book Praise and Worship Song Comments

*"Your message got me humming snatches of favorite old hymns for
a week or so, trying to decide which one I liked best... I find myself
defaulting to* **"Holy, Holy, Holy"** *when events start to leave me
agitated. I find that fixing my eyes firstly on the Lord provides that*

127

unmovable plumb line that causes everything around me to sort itself in order to right alignment."

"Praise is prayer! Thinking of, **"I Will Praise You in The Storm"** *by Casting Crowns and for some reason I've been walking around humming* **"Great is thy Faithfulness"** *... All I have need of thy hand hath provided!"*

"One that my husband and I like to dance to is a western song by Mercy Me **"Grace Got You"."**

"To God Be The Glory" *... Great Things He Has Done – "My husband and I went to a BSF leaders' Retreat at Glorietta. All the men and women were together in the auditorium to sing before the lecture... when the song began, you wouldn't believe the beautiful music we made... all our voices blended together to praise God. I thought, "this is the closest thing we can get to heaven without being In Heaven. "Every one of us were Christians singing praises to God. There may have been 300–400 of us .. it was beautiful!!"*

"The Love of God" *– "This is another BSF song. I had never heard this song before and we sang it in leader's meeting.. when we came to the 3rd verse, I was in tears.. we cannot describe God's love for us.. there's not enough ink in the ocean, there's not enough parchment. Even if every quill were a pen and every man a scribe.. not enough paper, ink, quill, or men to write about God's love."*

"My all-time favorite worship song is, **"How Great Thou Art"."**

"Ava Maria" ... *"So many times I've called upon Christ's mother for understanding."*

"The following have meant a great deal to me in my love and joy of Christ. **"Give Me Jesus"**, **"There Is a Place For Me at the Foot of the Cross"**, **"A Mighty Fortress"**, **"Ode to Joy"**.*"*

"Life Song by Casting Crowns" ... *"I love it because it reminds me that I want my life and my every day choices to represent and glorify Him, and to leave a legacy of faith for my girls to see."*

"Here is my favorite and why:

When I began attending BSF I was not born again. One part of the gathering that really touched me was the beauty of hearing that large number of women sing and joining in with them. Soon I began to notice that a particular song's lyrics were very interesting and I loved the concept of Christ being a solid rock to stand on because my life was sifting sand at the time. So, every time we sang **"THE SOLID ROCK (MY HOPE IS BUILT ON NOTHING LESS)"**, *it touched a deep longing in my soul. After about 6 months in BSF, through the power of the Word and its proclamation in reading and song, the truth penetrated my soul and the Holy Spirit breathed life into me. Praise God! So, when I sing that song or play it on the keyboard at church, my spirit rejoices in the true meaning of Christ, the Solid Rock!"*

"These first three really stir my heart to the reality of Jesus Christ and what He did for me and the last two are of course, old classics, but the words still ring as true today as they were then."

PRAYER BOOK PRAISE AND WORSHIP SONGS

1. Amazing grace
   Tomlin, Chris. "Amazing Grace (My Chains Are Gone)."
   YouTube video, 4:26. January 13, 2015
   https://www.youtube.com/watch?v=3MZgXXUW08Q
2. In Christ Alone
   Townend, Stuart. "In Christ Alone." YouTube video, 5:41.
   August 14, 2009.
   https://www.youtube.com/watch?v=RCeSOY5tisI
3. Raise a Halleluiah
   Helser, Jonathan & Melissa. "Raise a Hallelujah." YouTube
   video, 6:14. April 10, 2020.
   https://www.youtube.com/watch?v=YAMmrpXg7w4
4. How Great Is Our God
   Tomlin, Chris. "How Great is Our God." YouTube video,
   4:24. September 10, 2009. https://www.youtube.com/
   watch?v=cKLQ1td3MbE
5. Revive Us
   Mark, Robin. "Revive Us." YouTube video: 10:00. June 7, 2014.
   https://www.youtube.com/watch?v=KiOnBR-u-a8

6. Praise You in the Storm

   Casting Crowns. "Praise You in This Storm." YouTube video, 5:03. January 13, 2020. https://www.youtube.com/watch?v=0YUGwUgBvTU&feature=share&app=desktop

7. Grace Got You

   Mercy Me. "Grace Got You." YouTube video, 3:36. December 20, 2017 https://www.youtube.com/watch?v=xtiUjNT_vAM

8. Turn Your Eyes Upon Jesus

   Smith, Michael W. "Turn Your Eyes Upon Jesus." YouTube video, 3:13. October 28, 2012 https://www.youtube.com/watch?v=jMYZICnV2Ys

9. Bless the Lord Oh My Soul

   Redman, Matt. "10,000 Reasons (Bless the Lord o my Soul)." YouTube video, 4:21. January 25, 2014 https://www.youtube.com/watch?v=vSxocnIaN0A

10. Forgiveness

    West, Matthew. "Forgiveness." YouTube video, 4:25. July 9, 2012. https://www.youtube.com/watch?v=h1Lu5udXEZI

11. The Revelation Song

    Jobe, Kari. "Revelation Song – Passion 2013. YouTube video, 8:13. January 9, 2013. https://www.youtube.com/watch?v=3dZMBrGGmeE

12. How Great Thou Art

    Rice, Chris. "How Great Thou Art." YouTube video, 4:54. February 15, 2009. https://www.youtube.com/watch?v=Cc0QVWzCv9k

13. His Eye is On the Sparrow

    Selah. "His Eye is On the Sparrow." YouTube video, 3:34. October 17, 2017

    https://www.youtube.com/watch?v=ku2RUdcku_w

14. Lord I Lift Your Name on High

    Maranatha Singers. "Lord I Lift Your Name on High." YouTube video, 3:49. 2009

    https://www.youtube.com/watch?v=zVqWEtfpTgo

15. This is Amazing Grace

    Wickham, Phil. "This is Amazing Grace (Official Lyric Video)." YouTube video, 4:29. July 22, 2013

    https://www.youtube.com/watch?v=rjXjkbODrro

16. Good Good Father

    Tomlin, Chris. "Good Good Father ft. Pat Barrett." YouTube video, 4:19. February 18. 2020.

    https://www.youtube.com/watch?v=qlsQrycKKsY

17. Blessed Assurance

    Chapman, S.C. "Blessed Assurance." YouTube video, 4:21. April 2, 2013

    https://www.youtube.com/watch?v=jWJb0g0LhR0

18. Life Song

    Casting Crowns. "Lifesong" (Official Lyric Video). YouTube video, 5:20. February 3, 2020.

    https://www.youtube.com/watch?v=oEhlwljvOq0

19. I Surrender

    Hillsong UNITED (feat. Lauren Daigle). "I Surrender." YouTube video, 6:52. Empires Tour, 2016.

    https://www.youtube.com/watch?v=A4N2ausO6Sw

20. The Solid Rock

Hillsong Live. "Cornerstone (with lyrics) (worship with tears 31)." YouTube video, 6:47.

https://www.youtube.com/watch?v=nZq9xTfHvgo

21. Love Moved First

Casting Crowns. "Love Moved First (Official Lyric Video)." YouTube video, 3:26. May 7, 2020.

https://www.youtube.com/watch?v=Z8fWD_JpIFg

22. Rescue Story

Williams, Zach. "Rescue Story (Official Lyric Video)." YouTube video, 3:56. June 21, 2019.

https://www.youtube.com/watch?v=9Yr48Berkqc

23. So Will I

Hillsong UNITED. "So Will I (100 Billiion X) Official Lyric Video." YouTube video, 7:06. June 9, 2017

https://www.youtube.com/watch?v=oLURTvUQoTM

24. Give Me Jesus

Gokey, Danny. "Give Me Jesus (Live)." YouTube video, 5:55. January 22, 2016.

https://www.youtube.com/watch?v=bbh43MGoigw

25. Ave Maria

Bocelli, Andrea. "Ave Maria (SCHUBERT)." YouTube video, 5:55. July 11, 2009.

https://www.youtube.com/watch?feature=youtu.be&v=pwp1CH5R-w4&app=desktop

26. The Love of God

Mercy Me. "The Love of God (With Lyrics)." YouTube video, 3:38. 2002

https://www.youtube.com/watch?v=oWnvmKoLWUU

27. He is Everything to Me- A Capella
The Martins, A Capella. "He's Everything to Me." YouTube video, 2:09. July 24, 2018.
https://www.youtube.com/watch?v=O6DaBkMnNL8

28. We Will Remember
Walker, Tommy, "We Will Remember/From 'Break Through' (2006)." YouTube video: 5:05. February 23, 2017.
https://www.youtube.com/watch?v=qZzgeUJXmCM

29. What a Beautiful Name
Hillsong Worship. "What A Beautiful Name." YouTube video; 5:42. September 30, 2016.
https://www.youtube.com/watch?v=nQWFzMvCfLE

30. Still
Hillsong United. "Still with lyrics." YouTube video: 6:28. 2003.
https://www.youtube.com/watch?v=z3wwWFsSlNQ

31. Jesus I Need You
Hillsong Worship. "Jesus I Need You (2015 New Worship Song with Lyrics." YouTube video, 4:59. November 27, 2015
https://www.youtube.com/watch?v=Hfyyz1qtEZY

32. Here I Am to Worship
Hillsong Worship. "Here I Am to Worship/The Call." YouTube video, 6:28. August 3, 2017.
https://www.youtube.com/watch?v=6CKCThJB5w0

33. God Only Knows
For KING & COUNTRY. "God Only Knows (Officcial Music Video)." YouTube video, 4:22. July 26, 2018.
https://www.youtube.com/watch?v=Q5cPQg3oq-o

34. You Say
Daigle, Lauren. "You Say (Official Music Video." YouTube, 4:30. July 13, 2018.
https://www.youtube.com/watch?v=sIaT8Jl2zpI

35. When We Pray

Wells, Tauren. "When We Pray (Official Music Video)." YouTube video: 3:42. October 20, 2017. https://www.youtube.com/watch?v=9YZZzgJB33E

36. Move

TobyMac. "Move (Keep Walkin') (Lyric Video)." YouTube: 3:41. August 14,2015. https://www.youtube.com/watch?v=MX1G71WK-FA

37. Fear is a Liar

Williams, Zach. "Fear is a Liar (Official Live from Harding Prison)." YouTube, 4:39. October, 12, 2018 https://www.youtube.com/watch?v=e5LNfj2F5qI

38. The Old Rugged Cross

Jackson, Alan, "The Old Rugged Cross." YouTube, 3:06. April 18, 2015. https://www.youtube.com/watch?v=pClVtWjMBoY

39. The Lord's Prayer

Hillsong Worship, "The Lord's Prayer (Acoustic)-Hillsong Worship." YouTube, 4:43. October 10, 2018. https://www.youtube.com/watch?v=Du6GEXolWF0

40. I Just Need You

TobyMac, "TobyMac-I just need U." YouTube, 3:56. March 24, 2018. https://www.youtube.com/watch?v=BfbIoUMdKZ0

41. Oceans

Hillsong UNITED, "Oceans (Where Feet May Fall) Lyric Video-Hillsong UNITED." YouTube, 9:00. February 22, 2013. https://www.youtube.com/watch?v=dy9nwe9_xzw

42. Chain Breaker

Williams, Zach, "William Zach-Chain Breaker (Official Music Video)." YouTube, 3:48. October 24, 2016. https://www.youtube.com/watch?v=cd_xxmXdQz4

43. Great Is Thy Faithfulness

Austin Stone Worship, "Great is Thy Faithfulness Austin Stone Worship Live from TGC." YouTube, 6:56. July 18, 2018. https://www.youtube.com/watch?v=2eQ1oal44wU

44. Be Thou My Vision

NathanPachecoMusic, "BE THOU MY VISION-My Favorite Irish Hymn! :)." YouTube, 3:44. February 24, 2017. https://www.youtube.com/watch?v=ihJAJA4ibEs

45. Ode to Joy

Beethoven, Ludwig Van, "BEETHOVEN.ODE TO JOY." YouTube, 3:39. May 1, 2007. https://www.youtube.com/watch?v=Wod-MudLNPA

46. At the Foot of the Cross

Boltz, Ray, "AT THE FOOT OF THE CROSS-OFFICIAL VIDEO." YouTube, 3:59. November 3, 2012. https://www.youtube.com/watch?v=-gVUsTBQj_4

47. As the Dear

Maranatha Singers, "As The Deer- (With Lyrics)." YouTube, 4:06. December 21, 2008. https://www.youtube.com/watch?v=RVQmZCK4Fiw

48. Pass it On

Denolo, Nicole, "Pass It On-It only takes a spark (with subtitle)." YouTube, 3:01. August 5, 2013. https://www.youtube.com/watch?v=tadZ8nCLBsI

49. He Will Hold Me Fast

Getty, Keith & Kristyn, "Keith & Kristyn Getty- He Will Hold Me Fast (Official Lyric Video)." YouTube, 4:31. September 30, 2016. https://youtu.be/936BapRFHaQ

50. Trust and Obey

Moen, Don, "don moen TRUST AND OBEY." YouTube, 4:30. February 5, 2016.

https://www.youtube.com/watch?v=mVMwnWoqYnc

REFERENCES

Lockman Foundation., Zondervan 1987. *The Amplified Bible Containing the Amplified Old Testament and the Amplified New Testament.* Grand Rapids, Michigan: Zondervan.

Bounds, E.M. 1910. *Power Through Prayer.* Grand Rapids, Michigan: Baker Book House.

Chambers, O. 1989. *If You Will Ask.* Grand Rapids, Michigan: Discovery House.

Daniels., D.W. 2018. *51 Reasons Why the King James. Ontario, California: CHICK PUBLICATIONS.*

Haney, D. July 18, 2018. *Center for Healthy Churches. Baptist Standard. Commentary: Singing is praying twice.* Retrieved from: https://www.baptiststandard.com/opinion/other-opinions/singing-is-praying-twice/

Henry, M. 1917. *Matthew Henry's Commentary on the whole Bible.* Fleming H. Revell Company: New York, London and Edinburgh.

Holmes, K. March 15, 2019. *Be Still doesn't mean what you think it does...* INSPIRED TO FAITH. Retrieved from: https://www.inspiredtofaith.com/2019/03/15/be-still-doesnt-mean-what-you-think-it-does/

Jowett, J.H. *The Grace Awakening,* C. Swindoll, Word, 1990, pp. 140-41.

Killinger, J. 2012. *Beginning Prayer.* Nashville, Tennessee: Upper Room Books.

Korn, B. April 13, 2016. *7,000 Promises!! God's Light Christian Counseling. Retrieved from: https://godslightcc.wordpress.com/2016/04/13/7000-promises/*

Laurie, G. December 4, 2019. *Sow Your Blessing. Faith over Feelings.* Retrieved from: https://sowyourblessing.blogspot.com/2019/12/faith-over-feelings-greg-laurie-daily.html

Lewis, C.S. August 25, 2018. *Christian Fellowship. Treasures. Prayer.* Kenval. https://kenvalfellowship.org/2018/08/25/prayer-5/

Lindsey, H. 1986. *Combat Faith.* New York: Bantam Books.

MacArthur, J. 2020. Shepherd's Conference 2020. *Grace Quotes.* Retrieved from: https://gracequotes.org/arthur-quote/john-macarthur/

MacDonald, G. 1947. C.S. Lewis (editor) *An Anthology: 365 Readings.* San Francisco: HarperOne (2010).

Miles, C.A. 1912. In the Garden. Philadelphia, Pennsylvania: Hall-Mack.

Niebuhr, R. October 23, 2020. *Serenity Prayer.* Accessed on October 23, 2020. Retrieved from: https://en.wikipedia.org/wiki/Serenity_Prayer

Piper, J. & Taylor, J. 2009. *Power of the Words and the Wonder of God.* Wheaton, Illinois: Crossway.

Robinson, H. 1982. *Jesus Blueprint for Prayer.* Nashville, Tennessee. Thomas Nelson, Inc.

Rogers, A. 1975. *How to Pray in the Spirit. Romans 8:26-27.* Retrieved from https://www.lightsource.com/ministry/love-worth-finding/how-to-pray-in-the-spirit-829840.html

Ryken, L. 2002. *The Word of God in English: Criteria for Excellence in Bible Translation.* Wheaton, Illinois: Crossway.

Scofield, C.I. 1945. *The Scofield Reference Bible. The Holy Bible Containing the Old and New Testaments, Authorized King James Version.* New York: Oxford University Press.

Smith, C. Calvary Chapel Gwinnett. *Prayer is Vital. Effective Prayer Life.* Accessed on September 14, 2020. https://ccgwinnett.com/prayers/

Sproul, R.C. 1984. *Effective Prayer.* Wheaton, Illinois: Tyndale House Publishers, Inc.

Sproul, R.C. 2009. *The Prayer of the Lord.* Sanford, Florida: Reformation Trust Publishing.

Spurgeon, S. 2006. *Free and Dying Love/The Life of Susannah Spurgeon. Morning Devotions.* Carlisle, Pennsylvania: Banner of Truth.

Stanley, C. 1992. *The Wonderful Spirit Filled Life.* Nashville, Tennessee: Thomas Nelson, Inc.

Strong, J., 1890. *NAS Exhaustive Concordance of the Bible with Hebrew-Aramaicand Greek Dictionaries.* LaHabra, California: The Lockman Foundation. (1981,1998). Lockman.org

Theime, R.B.Jr. 1961. *The Faith Rest Life.* Houston, Texas: R.B. Theime Jr. Bible Ministries.

Tozer, A.W. 1964. *The Incredible Christian: How Heaven's Children Live on Earth.* Chicago, Illinois: Moody Bible Institute of Chicago.

Waite, D.A., April 21, 2016. *DEFENDING THE KING JAMES BIBLE. biblefortoday.org.* Retrieved from: *http://biblefortoday.org/Articles/DefendingTheKJB.pdf*

Wilson, R.F. October 30, 2020. *Names of God AND TITLES: 9.Abba,Father. JesusWalk BIBLE STUDY SERIES. Retrieved from: www.jesuswalk.com/names-god/9-father.htm*

Wikipedia. October 30, 2020. *In the Garden (1912 Song).* WikipediA The Free Encyclopedia. Retrieved from: *https://en.wikipedia.org/wiki/In_the_Garden_(1912_song)*

CPSIA information can be obtained
at www.ICGtesting.com
Printed in the USA
JSHW012100290321
13030JS00002B/3